Finding God

Claudia Azizah Seise

بِسْمِ ٱللَّهِ ٱلرَّحْمَٰنِ ٱلرَّحِيمِ

Finding God

Claudia Azizah Seise

All Rights Reserved © 2024 by Daybreak Press

No part of this book may be reproduced or transmitted in any form or by any means, graphic, electronic or mechanical, including photocopying, recording, typing, or by any information storage retrieval system, without the permission of the publisher.

Published by:

Daybreak Press | 3533 Lexington Avenue North | Arden Hills, MN 55126

Online: www.rabata.org/daybreakpress/ | Email: daybreakpress@rabata.org

ISBN: 978-1-7345914-8-4

Library of Congress Control Number: 2024937558

Cover art by: Askanadi, askanadi.de

Cover design by: Hagar Diab, hagardiab.com

Design and typesetting by: scholarlytype.com

Printed in the United States of America

To my teachers, known and unknown.
May Allah reward you all from His abundance! Ameen.

Contents

Author's Note	xi
Part One	1
The Turner of Hearts	3
Friday Prayer	7
Like Mother, Like Daughter	10
Sound of Faith	14
Muslim Hospitality	17
My First Ramadan	20
Change	25
Dialogue with Mother	32
Falling of Fears	39
From Kingdom Hall to the Ka'ba	43
Prosperity and Purpose	47
What's in a Name?	50
Islam All Around	53
A Family Affair	56
I Found God in the Australian Bush	60
Azizah's Choice	63
Islam in the USA	68
How Education Brought Me to Islam	72
Romancing the Faith	75
I Felt His Words	79
From the Nunnery to Islam	83
Living Religious Freedom, Living Islam	88
Kindness	91
Inspired by Islam Since Childhood	94

Contents

From Fame to Faith	97
I Went to Help Refugees, but They Helped Me	100
Losing it All	103
I Used to Believe in a New Prophet, Then I Found Islam	106
Monotheism for Life	110
I Saw Angels	114
I Ran Toward the Mosque	118
Science Points to the Existence of God	121
Out of the Mouths of Babies	124
Why Didn't Anybody Tell Me?	128
I Became Muslim to Get Married, Then Allah Opened My Heart	131
A French Convert	134
Finding God	136
Part Two	137
What Does It Mean to Be a Convert?	139
How to Find Your Place	142
Wisdom and Hope in Dealing with Your Non-Muslim Family	146
Letter to Non-Muslim Parents	149
Find a Gardener for Your Soul	152
Express Lanes on the Spiritual Path	161
Be Part of the Body	163
The Real Spirit of Spiritual Growth	168
We Are Women of God	171
Allah, Islam, and Our Priorities	174
A Mercy for the World	177
My Muslim Name	180
Getting the Right Balance	183
How Knowledge Can Make Us More Spiritual	186
How to Find Sweetness in Prayer	190
Letter to the Beloved	194
About the Author	199

Acknowledgments

My own learning with different teachers of the Muslim spiritual tradition heavily inspired the teachings and ideas in part two of this book. I am deeply indebted to Ustadha Mutia Fathiar (my first tajwīd teacher), Anse Dr. Tamara Gray, Dr. Umar Faruq Abdullah, Alimah Sobia Ahmed, Shaykh Kamaluddin Ahmed, my teachers at Rabata, Kyai Abdul Muhaimin, my teachers in Indonesia, Malaysia, & in other countries, & all the wonderful Muslim brothers & sisters who, without them knowing, became my teachers in this beautiful faith.

Author's Note

Bismillahir Rahmanir Rahim

With the Name of the Most Compassionate, the Most Merciful

I witness that there is no deity except God and that Muhammad is His Messenger. May Allah shower His blessings and peace upon His last and final Prophet, Muhammad.

It is now more than 20 years since I stood in my room in a Berlin flat and felt for the first time that I wanted to bow down to my Creator. Born into an atheist family in former East Germany, I had searched for my spiritual home since my early teenage years. I had a spiritual gap that nothing and no one else could fill, no matter what I tried. From that poignant moment in my old Berlin bedroom, it was several more years before God turned my heart to Him fully, but ever since, it has been an amazing journey toward Him and toward His pleasure—a journey that is filled with love, joy, hope, challenges, and many things to learn. A process of learning to trust God, to trust His absolute and complete knowledge again and again. A process of acknowledging my complete dependence upon Him. A journey where I found the peace, tranquility, and spiritual home I had searched for. A journey where I learned about myself, my role, and my purpose in this world. A journey to learn to accept what God has decreed for me.

Finding God is a part of this journey. This collection of convert stories began with writing my own story. Many converts know

Author's Note

that heritage Muslims and others are often eager to learn about a person's journey to Islam, so I had plenty of experience in sharing my story. Sometimes I had only two minutes in an elevator to sum up my years-long search for my spiritual home. Other times, I had an hour to tell the same story to an audience. Likewise, my story could be told in 500 words or a whole 300-page novel filled with color and feeling. But the 500-word convert story has the potential of moving many more hearts, because not everybody has the time or inclination to read a 300-page novel. So I started writing short convert stories of people I met or heard of, some of which were initially published on the website www.aboutislam.net. I looked for stories that also conveyed important spiritual teachings which, when we implement them in our everyday lives as Muslims, can become a reason for others to embrace Islam. Between 2018 and 2020, I collected and wrote more than forty stories, some of which form the first part of this book.

While teaching at the International Islamic University in Malaysia, I noticed that my students craved spiritual connection in addition to the academic curriculum. I decided to begin my classes with a short spiritual topic. I also began working with young converts, and observed a need for a more specific type of convert care. I was inspired to focus on convert-related topics after meeting Dr. Tamara Gray, founder of Rabata (rabata.org), in Malaysia in 2018. The second part of this book includes a collection of my writings for converts and Muslims in general. This second part can be read on its own or as a companion to the first part. Converting to Islam and finding one's place in their new community is an ongoing process, and the second part of this book provides tips and solutions to particular issues new Muslims might face, while also offering some thoughts on how all of us can draw nearer to God in everyday life through concrete deeds and worshipful reflection.

I thank God ﷻ and Daybreak Press for the opportunity to make these writings available to a broader audience. I also thank

Author's Note

my teachers who, consciously or not, guided me on this path of drawing nearer to Him. I ask God ﷻ to forgive any mistakes and shortcomings. May He make this book a means of bringing people, including myself, closer to Him. May He shower His blessings and peace upon our Prophet Muhammad ﷺ. *Ameen*.

Part One

Taking the First Step

The Turner of Hearts

This is the story of how I personally found God and accepted Islam. I've tried to focus on the moment I truly felt in my heart that God exists. Reflecting on my life after this realization, it seems that it was just a matter of time before God guided me to understand that it was Islam that explained how He wants us to worship Him.

I'm sitting in the huge mosque of the International Islamic University in Malaysia, listening to the *adhan*, the call to prayer. Tears fill my eyes. I cannot believe that Allah تبارك وتعالى has brought me here and allowed me to hear the call to prayer five times a day, seven days a week. My heart is filled with overflowing gratitude that makes it difficult to breathe. *Allah saved me again*, I think over and over. And I pray that all of us sitting in this mosque and every member of the Muslim *ummah* will reach the success that Allah calls us to in every single *adhan—falah!* Victory! And I bow down to Him, my Creator, my intimate Friend.

It has been more than 14 years since Allah moved my heart to accept His call. I don't know why He chose to grant me guidance or why He put the light of Islam in my heart. Why He chose this young woman from an atheist family, from the former communist East Germany, to bow down to Him. But I ask the Turner of Hearts every day to keep my heart on His path.

When I was a child, there was no mention of God in our home. No cross anywhere, no statue of Mary or Jesus. We never went to church, and we never prayed to anyone or anything. Life was void of spirituality. We celebrated Christmas, but only because it was a German tradition. We had a Christmas tree, candles, and Christmas songs. Sometimes this instilled some form of thoughtful atmosphere in my heart, but I did not know how to express it and it never lasted.

My parents were educated by the communist-socialist regime of the former German Democratic Republic. As outstanding and promising students, they were sent to the Big Brother, Russia, to study language and Marxism-Communism for five years. Back home, they worked at the university. They were convinced that there was no God, and that religion was human-made—an opiate of the masses. They never discriminated against people who believed, but it was just not for them. My maternal grandmother was the one who still had some form of belief in her heart, and although she did not express it openly, she sometimes said that she prayed for us. She had that "sixth sense" that we often find in older believers. I always felt very comfortable in her home and in her presence, although she did not talk a lot. The spiritual vacuum in my home caused my heart to turn restless. The older I became, the heavier this restlessness felt in my whole being. I was looking, searching, screaming, crying for that restlessness to be cured. I was rebellious, unruly, ill-mannered. I secluded myself, walked barefoot in the icy rain to extinguish this restless fire inside me, and looked up to the sky again and again. During my last years of high school, I started traveling. I spent one year in the USA and took several road trips across the country. Restless. I went backpacking in Southeast Asia. Searching. One night in Laos, I stretched out on a straw mat and looked up into the dark sky. I had never seen so many stars. I felt the earth moving. Staring out into space, I just knew. I was so sure—I could feel it deep inside my heart—that there was a Higher Being. There was a Creator. There was somebody watching over me. I just knew it. In the middle of the jungle in Laos, I felt God.

A few days later, I traveled to the Mekong Delta in the south of Laos. I sat on the veranda of a little bamboo hut and looked at the magnificent Mekong River. The lifeline of Southeast Asia, a mother river. It was over 20 kilometers wide and filled with all the stories it had collected during its travels. I was stunned by this wondrous creation. The steady flow of light brown water streamed into my heart and flushed out the restlessness. It poured a message from its Creator into my heart. My certainty grew that there was a God. After these two spiritual experiences with Allah's creation, I began to earnestly and eagerly search for Him. I searched in the pagodas and teachings of Theravada Buddhism in Thailand and Cambodia so earnestly that, at one point, I wanted to become an apprentice in a Buddhist monastery. I looked for Him in the Balinese Hindu temples. I tried to come closer to Him through yoga and meditation. I met with different Christian sects. Meanwhile, the inferno of my restlessness became fierce, wild and intense, and yet I also felt tired. Tired of the world, tired of traveling. I felt my life was meaningless. I did not see why I should work, why I should strive for anything. I felt that I had tried, done, and seen everything. Nothing new satisfied me anymore. Nothing even temporarily filled the void.

It was during this time that I started reading bits and pieces of a German translation of the Qur'an, since all the other religions I had read about were out of the question for me for different reasons. To be honest, I just cherry-picked passages from Qur'an about women's issues, especially those about covering the body and hair, to assure myself that Islam was too far from my liberal, freedom-loving worldview. I do not know how it happened or why, but one day Allah, the Turner of Hearts, just turned my heart to Him. He extinguished the burning heat with the coolness of His

guidance. I sat on a prayer mat and mumbled the profession of faith. At that time, I did not know much about Islam. I did not know how to perform the ritual prayer or how to recite Qur'an, but I felt that Allah had cured the restlessness that had perturbed me for so long. *Alhamdulillah*, a new life had begun.

Friday Prayer

Mario's story struck me because it beautifully illustrates the diverse ways that Allah chooses to bring people to Islam. Many of us struggle to strike a balance between our obligatory rituals and our worldly duties. Friday prayer is a prime example of that struggle. When we make Allah and His religion our first priority, we never know how that choice may affect the people around us.

After I graduated from high school almost 20 years ago, I worked different jobs to finance my studies at the community college in my hometown near the Mexican border. One of my jobs was at a local gas station, where I usually worked night shifts. Musa worked the afternoon shift from noon to eight. One Thursday, Musa asked me if I could switch shifts with him the next day. I agreed, and on Friday at eight, he took my shift. The same thing happened the week after. I didn't mind, as it seemed he had something really important to take care of on Friday afternoons. However, when I asked him the following week whether he would like to switch shifts, he declined. I didn't think anything of it and just followed my own schedule that week. The next week, Musa took me aside and explained that our supervisor had come down on him for switching shifts with me. If he wanted to keep his job, Musa had to comply with the supervisor's instructions and work Fridays during the day. Over the next few weeks, whenever I saw Musa, he was quiet and seemed unhappy.

Friday Prayer

Then one Thursday, Musa told me that he was planning to quit because he was being forced to work Fridays and would not be able to attend his prayer. I was shocked. Musa wanted to quit his job because he couldn't attend a prayer?

"So why don't you go pray another day?" I asked him.

He replied that it wasn't possible. I didn't understand. He must have noticed my puzzled look because he explained that attending Friday prayer in congregation is an extremely important part of being Muslim.

"Muslim? I didn't know you were Muslim."

Musa just smiled. We said goodbye, and that was the last I saw of him for a long time.

Curiosity

The fact that Musa quit his job to be able to attend his prayer on Fridays made me think. I thought of my family as religious. I mean, we didn't go to church every Sunday, but my mom often recited small prayers. My family was Catholic, and my parents had come to the US years before. We celebrated Christmas, but I had never seen my parents read the Bible. So I realized religion didn't play a big role in our life. But for Musa, his religion seemed to play a big part in his life. I began to ponder: How could anything, especially something like a certain prayer, be more important than having a job that pays your bills?

I wanted to know more about Musa's religion, but back in those days it wasn't easy to find information on Islam, especially in a small border town. One day, I saw Musa downtown. I had already approached and greeted him before I realized it wasn't Musa.

"Sorry, Bro," I said to him. "I thought you were my old friend Musa." The guy smiled and said, "I know a guy named Musa." "Musa the Muslim?" I quickly asked. The guy started laughing. "Yes, Musa the Muslim."

He asked me how I knew Musa and how I knew that he was a Muslim.

"Are you Muslim?" he asked.

I shook my head and told him the whole Friday story. He asked me if I would like to sit down for tea and continue our talk. I was glad for the invitation. Over the next several months, Omar told me everything I wanted to know about Islam. He became my best friend and teacher.

No Compromises

One fine Friday, Omar invited me to join the Friday prayer. I reminded him that I wasn't a Muslim. He just smiled and said, "Not yet."

I joined him. I listened to the imam's talk and imitated the prayer positions. After it was all finished, I looked at Omar. I had butterflies in my stomach.

"I'm ready," I finally managed to say. "Then let's start," he replied. "Everybody is waiting."

Omar accompanied me to the front of the prayer room where the imam waited. I sat down and repeated the Arabic and English words after him. My *shahāda*. My profession of faith. Many Fridays have passed since that special one, and wherever I've worked, I've made sure that Friday is my day off. I don't make any compromises on my Fridays. That's what I learned from my friend Musa the Muslim.

Like Mother, Like Daughter

Many times we feel that we have to do something particular to introduce a person to Islam, like hand out flyers or engage in long religious discussions to convince the other person of the truth. Often these attempts fail to bear fruit. We tend to forget that just being a beautiful person, living our religion in the best way possible and treating others kindly, can be the best way to attract people—including our family members—to Islam.

When I was 13 years old, my mom embraced Islam. It was strange. You know, being 13...everything was new. My body changed, my moods changed, my outlook on life changed, and it was during that time of change that my mother decided to transform her life as well.

It wasn't easy for me to accept her decision. Our diet changed. We ate less meat because halal meat was difficult to get in our small town. I didn't like how people in the streets looked at my mom's head covering. And it was strange to eat alone when she fasted during Ramadan. She would listen to recitations of the Qur'an while I listened to music in my room.

No Compulsion

It was difficult for me to accept my mom's new way of life, and I was glad that she never pressured me to accept Islam. She started praying, but she never told me to pray. She started wearing the headscarf, but she never told me to wear it. Much later I learned that she was following the Islamic teaching that there is no compulsion in religion.

> *Let there be no compulsion in religion, for the truth stands out clearly from falsehood. So whoever renounces false gods and believes in Allah has certainly grasped the firmest, unfailing handhold. And Allah is All-Hearing, All-Knowing.* (Qur'an 2:256)

So, although I was young, she respected me and did not push me. She just incorporated Islam into her life. My mom's patient approach had a positive effect on me. I became curious about her new religion. I wanted to know about Islam, but I wanted to find it my own way. I guess my mom knew me very well. She knew that I had to come to Islam on my own. She knew the stubborn young woman I was. Later, after I joined her in accepting Islam, she told me how much she had prayed for me. How much she had begged Allah جَلَّ جَلَالُهُ to turn my heart to Him. She told me that she had gotten up almost every night before the morning prayer and made *du'a* for me.

Searching

After I finished high school, I went on to study Arabic and Islamic Studies at university. I wanted to know more about Islam, and I figured that it would be good to know Arabic. However, the Islamic Studies courses at the university were taught by non-Muslim academics, and they certainly did not help me better understand

Islam. I wanted to know about Allah, but they could not tell me anything about Him.

My questions were more spiritual. I wanted to know what it would mean to build a relationship with Allah, so I started reading books by Muslim authors and Islamic scholars from the past. Imam Al-Ghazali's tender and beautiful writings struck me the most and eventually led me to embrace Islam. More than 10 years after my mom had accepted Islam, I followed her. I didn't tell her at first because I didn't want her to think I had done it for her. I checked my heart again and again to see whether I had converted to please my mom or whether I had done it solely and purely for the sake of Allah ﷻ. I found that truly, I had not embraced Islam to please any human being. I knew that I wanted to be part of what Allah calls in the Qur'an "the best community."

> *You are the best community ever raised for humanity—you encourage good, forbid evil, and believe in Allah.* (Qur'an 3:110)

I wanted to change my life. I wanted the light of faith in my heart.

Sisters

When I finally told my mom that I had accepted Islam, she hugged me for what seemed like 10 minutes. Unrestrained tears rolled down my cheeks and I felt a connection with my mom that I had never felt before. We were now not only mom and daughter, but we were also sisters in Islam. We were not only connected in this world, but we would also be connected in the Hereafter, *insha Allah*. When my mom slowly loosened her hug, I saw that her cheeks were also wet with tears. We stood for a long moment, holding hands. Quiet.

Then my mom said, "Assalamu alaikum."

And I answered her greeting and *du'a* for eternal peace with: "Walaikum assalam."

Sound of Faith

Lisa was born in Austria and is now in her forties living and working in Malaysia. In her extraordinary narrative, we can see how Allah is able to turn a person's heart in a second. This change can be so profound that, as in Lisa's case, everything in life is turned upside down. But Allah takes care of the consequences in the most beautiful way.

I had lived close to a mosque for 10 years, yet the sounds coming from its loudspeaker had never affected me in any way. Then there came a day when the recitation of the Qur'an from the mosque was not just that usual background noise anymore. It was the month of Ramadan, and I could hear the imam recite Qur'an during the *tarawīh* prayer every night. I felt an irresistible inclination toward the recitation. I wanted to hear more of it. So, although I wasn't Muslim, I bought a CD to be able to listen to it whenever I wanted.

Despite living in a Muslim-majority country, I worked at a Catholic university and neither my husband nor I were Muslim. Converting to Islam had never even crossed my mind. But I continued listening to the recitation of Qur'an, by myself, after Ramadan was over. It lent so much peace and contentment to my soul. Whenever I was free, I turned to it. I didn't understand a word, and yet the Qur'an calmed my mind. I felt at peace. It was exactly what I needed to soothe my restless heart.

Alone

One quiet night, the urge to connect to this beautiful recitation became unbearably strong. I wanted to be part of the community of people who held it dear. I wanted to connect to the Being whose words had lifted my heart. I wanted to feel that peace and contentment in every moment of my life. I wanted the Qur'an to fill me. In the quietness of the night, I sat down on the floor and there, one on one with Allah, I recited my *shahāda*. I did not tell anybody about my secret relationship with Allah for two years. I kept it hidden from everybody, for I was afraid that it would be spoiled and stained by other people's judgments. I wanted my relationship with Allah to grow, to become strong, and to become so intense that no ugly comment or hurtful gesture would come between me and my Lord. I prayed secretly. I studied Qur'an secretly on the internet. I learned about my new religion and my Lord through reading.

Teacher

After two years, I felt that my connection with Allah had become unshakable. I felt strong and filled with His light. It was then that I began learning about Islam with a religious teacher at an Islamic school. Every Saturday and Sunday, I studied traditional religious books with her. I became a primary school student in Islam. I learned the very basics, like how to purify myself for prayer, how to approach my Lord, and how to beautify my behavior toward my teacher and toward people in general.

I moved in with a Muslim lady teacher after my husband made a clear statement that he did not want to embrace Islam. I still tried to convince him, but I wound up asking for a divorce when it became clear he did not want to accept Islam. Living and learning at my teacher's home connected me with many other students of Islam.

Most were much younger than I, but what connected us all was our love and passion for Allah's religion. I learned to read Qur'an and memorized parts of it. Every new word, every new piece of knowledge, brought me closer to my Lord.

Covering

It was also during this time that I started covering my hair on a daily basis. Praise be to my most merciful Creator, even at my Catholic workplace people accepted my decision, my new life, and my new look! Allah opened their hearts and guided them to accept me for who I am.

One of the most beautiful things in my life now is being able to listen to the recitation of Qur'an while standing in prayer at the mosque. It is during these moments that I feel the tremendous gift Allah تَبَارَكَ وَتَعَالَى has bestowed upon me and upon all of humanity.

Muslim Hospitality

Hospitality is a very important principle in Muslim teachings and Muslim cultures all over the world. The story of Andreas Ahmad, who embraced Islam over twenty years ago in Germany, beautifully illustrates how this sunna of honoring the guest can serve as a means to open a person's heart to Islam.

It was during my last two years of high school that I made friends with one of my classmates. He usually sat by himself and didn't talk much. I was similar. One day we started chatting during lunch, and from that day forward we spent our lunch breaks together. One day in early fall, Hasan arrived at lunchtime but didn't eat. He just sat and watched me eat. It was kind of strange, but I didn't question him at first. When it continued like that for the whole week, though, I finally asked him why he wasn't eating lunch. I suspected he didn't have the money and I wanted to help him out. But he politely declined my offer and told me he was fasting. Then he invited me home to have dinner with his family.

Being a Guest

That evening, his mother greeted me like I was her own son. I felt a bit awkward at first, but their openness and the festive atmosphere helped me relax and enjoy myself. Hasan's grandparents were also there. I remember asking whether they came to visit often. Hasan's mother just laughed and said that they all lived together. I couldn't believe it. I rarely saw my grandparents, although they lived only two hours from us.

Hasan's mother called everybody to the dinner table, which was overflowing with delicious sweets and new-to-me dishes. I was served first, and Hasan's father filled my cup with tea every time I finished it. I was so comfortable that I didn't want to go back home! There, we never had dinner together. Everyone just grabbed something from the fridge when they felt hungry. We almost never had guests, and if I brought a friend home, my mother made sure he left before dinner time. It became a beautiful ritual that once a week Hasan would invite me over for dinner. It was always the best day of my week. Every time I visited, they treated me like a king. I started to wonder why there was such a stark difference between my family and Hasan's. At that time, Islam was not an issue in the news, so I didn't realize that Hasan was Muslim. Although I did always wonder why his mom hid her hair under a colorful scarf.

I Want That

Finally, one day I worked up the courage to ask Hasan why his mom always covered her head. He patiently explained. The next time I visited, I stayed a bit longer than usual. It was then that I saw the whole family pray together. That *really* stirred my soul. They not only had dinner together, but they also turned toward God together. And they treated me, their guest, in such a beautiful way. They made me feel like they genuinely cared about me. I wanted more of that in my life. I wanted to be like them. The next day when I met Hasan at lunchtime, I asked him about the prayer and what I would have to do to be like them. So, after school, we went to his house and waited for his dad to come home from work. Hasan told him that I wanted to become Muslim. His dad gave me a surprised, happy hug. We sat down on a prayer mat, and he instructed me on how to read the *shahāda*.

It is now more than 20 years since I embraced Islam. I have moved away from my hometown and have a family of my own. Hasan's family is still very dear to me. They showed me the beauty of Islam and the excellent way our Prophet Muhammad ﷺ taught us to treat our guests. It was their beautiful behavior that called me to Islam.

My First Ramadan

This account relates my very own first experience of Ramadan. It illustrates in a very personal way that conversion does not stop after accepting Islam, but is an ongoing process, and that Ramadan, as one of Islam's five pillars, is always a time to grow.

It is the first day of Ramadan in the Muslim year 1429, or 2008 in the Gregorian calendar. Monday, the first of September. I have been nervous for weeks, always asking myself the same question, giving myself the same answers, and fighting with fears that are probably incomprehensible to others.

What if I get hungry—or even worse, thirsty? What if I'm not strong enough? If I can't do it? If I get sick? Where should I draw the line between bearing the suffering and giving up?

Someone who has always fasted between sunrise and sunset during Ramadan is used to it. She is probably unable to relate to my confusion, which is caused by both inner and outer pressures. "Just try," and "Don't pressure yourself," are easy words for lifelong Muslims to say, but I'm totally new and I feel alone in this.

Not Even Water?

I had become a Muslim about six months earlier. Fasting during the month of Ramadan was an issue for me from the beginning—the one pillar of Islam that I would have liked to skirt around. I wished I could just ignore it. I just could not imagine going a whole day without eating and especially without drinking. I have always been afraid of not getting enough to drink, afraid of getting headaches or other strange indispositions. And now I would not be allowed to drink anything at all during the daytime for the next four weeks. Impossible!

Fears

My anxiety grew with every passing day. My mother's cautions rang in my head: didn't I remember what happened to me when I couldn't eat on time and had to go hungry for a while? Headaches, attacks of nausea, bad temper.

"Is it *really* necessary to put yourself through all that?" she asked.

And honestly, I didn't know what to say.

I knew that fasting was one of the five duties of every Muslim, and I also knew that elderly or ill people, or women having difficult pregnancies, were exempted, or allowed to make up their fasts at a later date, but I did not belong to any of those groups. I was still young and healthy.

Panic is probably the best word to describe my emotional state during those weeks before my first Ramadan. I was a pain for the people around me, always bothering them with the same questions that were designed to calm my mind: What if? Do I have to? Why? Always getting the same unsatisfying answers. In the end, I surrendered to destiny. No, actually I decided to just try it, believing that God would stand by me.

Prepping

Alongside the nerves, though, was the excitement. I was looking forward to stocking up enough food and drinks to consume during the hours before sunrise—*suhūr* time—but I couldn't think of anything I would be able to eat in those early morning hours except rice with eggs. So I made sure I ate that. I also bought fresh milk and honey because one of my neighbors had told me that she always drank milk in the morning during the fasting month.

A few days earlier, I had bought a rice cooker so I could both cook rice and keep it warm. That way I was able to boil it in the evening and avoid standing in the kitchen cooking at three o'clock in the morning.

The Night Before

The night before the first fasting day, I was preparing food for the morning, when suddenly I was standing in complete darkness. I was confused, uncertain, and desperate and all the other words one can think of in such a situation. I sat on the veranda and stared into the darkness, unable to cry over such a tiny incident but too desperate to laugh, either. I had no other idea how to express my feelings at that moment. Emotional exhaustion triggered by a power failure.

Luckily, my neighbor was able to deduce that it was just the fuse. Unfortunately, there was only one in the whole house. (And it had probably been the rice cooker that caused it to blow!) But for a few moments, there I was—completely convinced that the electric company had cut my electricity the night before the first of Ramadan on purpose—revenge because I was often late paying my bills! An hour later we had bought a new fuse and, after some trying, it worked. I was able to eat my rice and eggs before the Fajr *adhan*. The first day, the second, and the third passed, and

I still fasted. Honestly, it was especially hard in the first few days after breaking my fast in the evenings. My body just suddenly ran out of its emergency power supply, and all I wanted was to sleep instantly, at seven in the evening. In Ramadan, your body must adjust not only to the lack of food and drink, but also to an abbreviated sleep schedule. That lack of sleep makes the first few fasting days a real challenge.

I didn't get headaches as many people do, I did not feel ill, and I was not bad-tempered. In this regard, I was honestly surprised. I was not even hungry, and only in the late afternoon hours, around one hour before breaking the fast, did I get thirsty. A miraculous blessing of Ramadan.

The Colors of Fasting

I have always visualized things in terms of color. And I had imagined fasting in all the gray and black shades I could find in my consciousness. Suffering, pain, and suffering again. Thankfully, none of that happened—at least not at the physical level. But that does not mean that fasting boasts bright, loud colors like red, yellow, or green, either. At least not for me.

Rather, I experienced fasting as almost transparent colors. Like one would find in great heights, in the silence and loneliness of the mountains. Soft, floating beige, a fading ochre shade, a dissolving violet-gray. Colors that are removed from any worldliness. Colors without lust and greed. Colors of pure being. Through these colors, I understood that the fasting month belongs to God سُبْحَانَهُ وَتَعَالَى.

Cleansing Process

The first two weeks I felt light, but deeply rooted in myself and in the world—a lightness and openness for the things that lay ahead of me that I had never felt before. Devotion to the present. Closeness to God. These are the best descriptions I can find, although I know they are the most difficult to understand. Abstract.

In the second half of the fasting month, however, something radically changed in my mental state. I became quickly irritated. My senses, especially my hearing, were oversensitive, and a dissatisfaction with myself and my surroundings seemed to grow with every day. It was like the poison, the toxins, and the garbage that had left my body during the previous two weeks had congregated in my psyche, ready to exit with such force and ruthlessness that they did not consider the person behind it all—me. I saw it coming. I felt it building up. It was boiling in me. Then one day I felt an explosive breakdown rushing toward me, and I could do nothing to stop it. It was like a part of me had detached itself and was now being forced to leave my body, like an overgrown boil that was being lanced, releasing putrid, bloody pus. That's how my breakdown felt. I could only wait for it to pass, until all the bitter, noxious tears had left me. I still felt weak and incomplete a few days after this event, but then the place that had been occupied by the inflamed boil filled itself with something new—a strength, a balance, and a bright, glowing love that made me quickly forget the breakdown. After one month of fasting, I was glad to pick up my regular daily activities again, but I would never wish to have missed the intense, challenging, and spiritual experience that was my first Ramadan.

Change

We are often unaware of the impact our conduct has on other people. Many times we are caught up in our own little world, occupied with our personal challenges to the extent that we do not take note of what happens around us. This way of walking through life prevents us from living in the moment and following our greatest example, our beloved Prophet Muhammad ﷺ. Diana's story is a detailed account of her path to Islam through both academic research and personal encounters with Muslim women who were beacons of light in hijab.

The change happened during one of my last semesters at university, where I had studied gender and anthropology. I remember I was a hardcore feminist at the time—at least that's what everybody said. I had specialized in female role models in Southeast Asian societies and was preparing my final thesis on Muslim women in Indonesia, which included field work in Java. To be honest, I had prepared for my upcoming research visit with a notion of pity for those poor Indonesian women who had to wear a headscarf (*jilbāb* in Indonesian) every time they went out into the tropical heat. I felt sorry for them because they had to suffer near heatstroke instead of just letting their beautiful, shiny black hair loose. And there were other things related to Muslim dress regulations, especially for women, that I felt ambivalent about. As a result, I was anxious that I did not possess the necessary distance one needs to assume the more-or-less neutral position of a researcher. I shared my concerns with my thesis supervisor, one of the first women to obtain a doctoral degree in gender studies and an active member of the women's movement. This woman, whom I considered an almost radical feminist, told me that I had to keep an open mind, control my stereotypes, and leave my preconceptions at home if I ever wanted to understand women's reasons for wearing a headscarf.

"Don't bring your anti-male attitude with you. Who knows? Maybe Indonesian women decide by themselves whether they want to wear the headscarf or not. Don't automatically assume they are being forced by their husbands or fathers," she said.

She gave me that smile I had learned to recognize—the one that meant my consultation time was over.

Confusion

Confused and somehow disillusioned, I walked through the streets of Berlin. Everything my supervisor had said I had already known intellectually, but I did not know how to transfer it to reality. This research was not about single mothers in Thailand, or prostitutes in Cambodia, or factory workers in Vietnam. I felt it was something much deeper, something that went beyond gender and women's role in society to something I had never dealt with before—spirituality. The unseen. Even God. I was close to panic. Why did I have to choose this topic? Why couldn't I just choose something normal, simple, less confusing? Something I was familiar with that didn't involve my own feelings, where I could just use all my gender theories without having to see the other side. Something I could easily judge through the window of my Western perspective, like women in Indian literature or female pop singers in Vietnam. Something easy. I was not ready to question my Western view of those "poor, suppressed Muslim women," and I was not ready

to question myself. I felt all that turmoil crouching behind the innocent word "research," ready to roll over me, ready to drown me in my own confusion.

I decided to give it all up. The next day I would talk to my supervisor. I would think of a different topic, something less scary. Yes, that was it. A little bit calmer, I entered the subway to go home.

Random Encounter

Riding the subway in Berlin is invariably an interesting experience. There is always something strange to see or exciting to observe. It can be both depressing and uplifting. One hour on the Berlin subway can both illustrate the darkest side of the human soul and the utterly selfless, humanitarian side as well—selflessness you would never have suspected in the aloof faces of the people riding to work every morning.

Across from me sat a young Muslim woman. She was probably of Turkish origin, as most Muslims in Berlin are. The way she wore her hair high up below her headscarf, making her head look conical, almost like an egg, was typical of Turkish headscarf fashion in Berlin. She held a small pocket Qur'an in her hands, and her lips moved silently as she read. She seemed absorbed in her recitation and did not appear to notice my conspicuous stare. I could not take my eyes off her, and I started feeling the hot nervousness in my stomach that I usually experience when I am hesitant to speak up because I feel shy, embarrassed, or uncertain of what I am about to say. I wanted to know then and there: did she wear the headscarf because it was really her personal choice, or was she made to wear it by her authoritative father or fanatical husband? But how was I supposed to approach her, disturb her in her recitation? When my stop came, I decided to skip it. My nervousness developed into nausea. My heart beat faster, and I felt ridiculous sitting in front of her, not being able to act or move. Had I chosen the Vietnamese pop singers, nothing like this would have happened. I would not have even had to go to Vietnam. Berlin-Marzahn would be far enough to look for them. There are dozens of them in Vietnam Town, as that part of Berlin is informally called. While my thoughts raced in all directions, I did not notice that the Turkish woman was looking at me, smiling. She seemed to glow in the fake daylight of the subway. In perfect German, she asked me if I was alright. I could only nod my head, embarrassed. I must have looked totally disturbed. With a shaky voice that sounded like it came from somewhere outside my body, I said, so as to excuse myself, "I just wondered why you wear the headscarf. Do you want to?"

For a moment she appeared confused, but then quickly answered: "Yes, I want to. It is my personal choice, as an expression of my belief and what is written in the Qur'an about female modesty."

I was baffled, but smiled and thanked her for her openness. Just when she was about to step out of the subway, I called after her, "You really helped me. Thank you."

That afternoon I spent another two hours in my seat, unable to get off the subway because I was afraid to lose the light this Muslim woman had lit in my mind.

In Indonesia

Three weeks later, I arrived at Adisutjipto International Airport, Yogyakarta. I would spend the next three months researching for my master's thesis. Yogyakarta is a very inspiring town, full of culture and tradition, art, and education. People from all over Indonesia meet in Yogyakarta to celebrate the diversity that makes the town such a special place. I noticed quickly that Yogyakarta was the right place to do my research because I was able to talk to both

local women and women from all over Java, Sumatra, Sulawesi, and even West Papua. That gave me the opportunity to base my research on Indonesian Muslim women, not just Javanese or Yogyakartan women. I interviewed over 30 Muslim women—some young, some old, but all of them wearing the *jilbāb*. Some wore plain black or white ones, some wore pink, yellow, red, or baby blue. Some even wore a veil that only revealed their eyes. Some did not even let their eyes show. Some wore their head covering loose, covering their bosoms, while others wore it tight so you could see the exact shape of their head and ears and the approximate length of their hair, the fabric drawn around their necks making them look like turtles. Some wore little brooches to hold the fabric in place. Some showed a little bit of hair covering their foreheads, but most did not. To make a long story short, the *jilbābs* worn in Indonesia come in all imaginable forms, colors, and sizes. Most of the women told me they wore the *jilbāb* because they wanted to, because it was a part of their religion. Others mentioned wearing it because their grandmothers and mothers wore it as well. That particular reason made the headscarf sound like part of Muslim Indonesian tradition, not part of Islam's regulations concerning women's dress. It felt to me like most of the women I interviewed did not reflect on why they or their grandmothers and their mothers wore the *jilbāb*.

Except for two women, none of them claimed they were forced to wear it. Except for one young woman, none of them seemed to be conscious of their own personal reasons for their donning the *jilbāb*. For them, it was enough that the Qur'an said that women had to cover their body except their faces and hands. No personal reflection or questioning entered it. I was a bit disappointed.

One Exception

Then I met Fithrie.

During our first meeting in public, I could only see her dark, profound eyes that seemed to look straight into my soul. Even with everything else covered, I found her amazingly beautiful. There was a light shining through all the black cloth covering her from head to toe.

Here is what she told me:

> Covering myself gives me personal freedom because I am not reduced to a mere object of bodily beauty (you would say I am not a "sex object"). I do not feel disturbed by unwanted lecherous looks from men or unpleasant comments in the streets, and therefore I am able to keep my peace of mind and concentration. You know, I am a writer, so I almost constantly think about my projects, my current book, or an article for a magazine. Covering my body also brings me closer to God. Because men pay less attention to me, I feel removed from the burden of handling or being influenced by other people's sexual emotions. I feel somehow cleaner and more virtuous.
>
> I think covering one's beauty requires one to work harder to impress other people. Because people cannot see your outer appearance, they can only judge you by your words and actions. I know you, Western women, tend to view women like me with pity because we cannot or do not want to be free to show our bodies and impress other people with our beauty. But I think that what you call freedom is just a prison of physical appearances. You will never experience true personal freedom, detached from any outside judgment, because you will always stay on the physical level. You judge freedom on the physical level. That's what I want to escape. It is too simple, too plain. That is why I cover myself. Under my cover I can experience personal freedom.

Convinced

Her words struck me like a lightning bolt. This was exactly what I had been looking for…and what I had been so scared to hear. I knew she was right, but I could not admit it, nor could I argue with her. All my feminist theories, all my gender perspectives were worthless when confronting Fithrie. I knew this was the stuff I needed for my research, and I knew that after I had finished, I would not be the same person who had begun it. Fithrie's words made my own convictions and all I had learned about Western feminist ideas around personal freedom seem so rudimentary, so obscene and superficial.

I no longer wished I had chosen to write about Vietnamese pop singers.

When, half a year later, I went to my supervisor's office to hand in my final thesis—without any further consultation after I had finished my research in Indonesia—she could not hide her surprise.

"I see that your thesis includes a Muslim feminist approach. I was not sure how your research would go, but honestly, I did not expect to see you like this."

I wore a plain black headscarf that draped modestly over my chest.

Dialogue with Mother

No matter our decisions or circumstances, we should always make an attempt to preserve family ties and keep our relatives close to us. This can take courage, patience, and perseverance. Sara's story relates the difficulties she experienced when telling her mother of her choice to embrace Islam.

I was nervous. I had been nervous ever since I admitted to myself that I would have to tell my mother. It was just that I could not decide how to tell her. Straightforwardly? Maybe that would cause too much emotion, too much irritation and unnecessary arguments. Maybe I should not tell her in person but write her a letter or an email, put all my thoughts and feelings in written words and then wait and see what happens. But what if my mother misunderstood or misinterpreted? Then my problem would be bigger than before. No, it would be better to be able to observe her reactions, see her eyes, and hear the intonation of her voice.

But just the thought of sitting in front of my mother made my mouth feel dry and my hands cold and sweaty. Maybe I should ask my younger sister to assist. Frida already knew everything. I had told her the whole story, all the ins and outs, and had explained all the whys and rejected all the buts. In the end, Frida had accepted it and had even started to like the thought of my change. She surprised me with interesting, challenging discussions. Our years apart had changed Frida from a spoiled, sometimes annoying, often bad-tempered teenager to a mature and thoughtful young woman who was open to the colorful facets of life's challenges and surprises.

I was proud of Frida and glad that our often-difficult relationship had taken a better turn. Yes, I would ask her to stand by me when the time came to reveal my secret to my mother.

Dreams

I arrived late at night. The flight from Malaysia took over twenty hours, with a layover in Dubai. I was jet-lagged and exhausted; even though I had wanted to use the time on the plane to get some rest, I could not make myself go to sleep. Each time I started drifting into that space between awake and asleep, my mind started playing a terrifying scene with my mother. I had had the same dream night after night. Each time, I was sitting in my mother's living room waiting for her to come home from work.

Those moments of waiting always made me feel incredibly anxious and worthless and I would ask: "Who am I to add problems to my mother's life? Why don't I just keep it to myself, let her live on without having to question the very pillars of her existence?"

Then my mother would appear. She would look weary and anxious, and I would be desperate to just tell her everything and get it over and done with. But before I could get the chance to do so, my mother would disappear.

But one night something new happened in this dream-like state...a new scene. While I tried to tell my mom about what had happened in my life, some invisible force pushed the sound of my voice back into my throat. When I then tried to say the words again, my mother's face changed. She became a different woman. At first, I thought it was the face of a stranger, but the longer I looked at her, the more familiar the new face became.

Just before I remembered the name of my mother's new face, the face started shouting and yelling in an inhuman, crow-like voice: "No Sara, you are wrong! Sara, you don't understand. There is no other interpretation to the story of the feeding of the ten thousand. You always think you know better! Why do you always have to disturb us with your uneducated questions? I know, I know, it's the devil that makes you ask those questions. The devil! Oh Jesus, help!"

I recognized the voice the minute my mother's face opened its mouth. It was my high school Bible Studies teacher. The one who had something scary and very dark around her. It was because of this teacher that I had dropped that subject and changed to morals and ethics studies. And now, when I wanted so much to finally find the courage to tell my mom about my new life, this woman's face appeared in my memory to try and shake my new balance and conviction.

Still dizzy and half asleep, I mumbled, "No Missus, you are the one with the devil. You tried to forbid me to think, to question, and to look behind the written word. You tried to forbid me to search for the truth."

I promised myself that the next time my former teacher appeared in my dream, I would talk back to her and make her forever disappear from my memory. But still, this dream kept me from resting and left me even more nervous. I silently prayed that my mother would not become like the hysterical face of Mrs. Tiedemann.

Worries and Fear

I was thankful that mom was unable to pick me up from the airport. I took advantage of the situation and decided to stay a few nights with a friend to readjust to life in Europe and gain some

moral support before meeting my mom and sharing the decision that had changed my entire life. When I arrived at my mom's, I sat in the living room just as in my dream and waited for her to come home from work. Over half a year had passed since I had decided what I was about to reveal to my mother. My younger sister had pushed me to come clean, and of course I knew I would have to tell my family eventually, but the subject was so fraught. It wasn't just about the telling. There was also the responsibility. I knew that I would be confronted with fear, misunderstanding, disbelief, and probably questions like "Is this really my daughter?"

I would really hate to see that question on my mother's face. It was perhaps fear of this silent question that shook me the most.

The Meaning of Muslim

In today's crazy Western world of terrorism and mass paranoia, pervasive ignorance, and a pretend-to-know society, becoming a Muslim is something most people are unable to comprehend, to put it the most polite way. In Malaysia, everybody was happy to hear that I had become a Muslim and followed the five pillars of Islam—or at least they accepted it politely. People often gave thanks to God when they found out.

The problem was that my mother did not believe in God. At least she claimed not to. Phrases like "that happened by accident," "by coincidence," or "surprisingly" were her explanations when something out of the ordinary occurred. I had never believed in chance or so-called accidents, even before I became a Muslim. Somehow, I always knew there was something that regulates it all. A divine power. God.

The Moment of Truth

When I sat in front of my mother, I wanted to explain all that. My feelings during childhood, the hollow emptiness, the ongoing search for what I had felt was missing in my life. But when I said "Mom, I'm a Muslim now," I could see the question, the question I feared most, starting to shine its grey light on my mom's face. "Is this really my daughter?"

But I did not want her to voice it, so I kept on talking and talking, trying to talk that question away—that question that would destroy my confidence and prevent me from ever feeling understood.

"But Sara, remember I rescued you from that weird Christian sect? You know, the ones with the circle and the strange voices?"

"I know, mom. But this time it's different. Oh, it is so different, Mom. I'm full of life and strength. I had to—", but she did not let me finish the sentence. My most important sentence.

"What about Buddhism? You were interested in Buddhism. That's a nice religion..." I knew what she was going to ask next, but I cut her off and with a convincing strength in my voice that surprised me and probably my mother and sister as well.

"Mom, Buddhism is probably the most discriminatory religion in the world, besides Hinduism and its caste system. Buddhism as it is known in Western countries is not the Buddhism found in Asia. The one in the Western world is a New Age religion for lost people in the West. The one in Asia teaches that spirituality and divine knowledge are reserved for a small group of men only—the monks. There are nuns, but they are more like servants or maids. Everybody else—lay men and women—are just sheep that follow this small group of "spiritually enlightened" people. They light incense and bring offerings and actually believe that God needs things like that. They don't pray to God, they pray to spirits,

ancestors, and ghosts, or *jinn* as we call them in Islam. Buddhism has been corrupted for centuries."

Did I Say Too Much?

My mother's face went blank. I knew I had said too much at once, but I couldn't stop, not at that essential turn of the conversation. Maybe she didn't understand at that moment, but later when she had time alone to think, she might understand.

"Mom," I continued in a soft, low voice. "Mom, I had to become a Muslim. There was no other choice for me anymore. I felt that I had found the truth, the real light, the reason why I am here in this world—the reason for my existence. Mom, I have never told you, but the last few years I have been seriously questioning myself and my existence. What is it all for? Why am I working hard? Why should I enjoy life? For what, Mom? I was on the verge of falling into a deep canyon of meaninglessness and nothingness. I felt my energy dwindling and my joy in life fading away. I could not point to a single reason to live. Now I know the reason, Mom. I know it. It is for God."

The Way to Understanding

The atmosphere in the room felt heavy and indescribably quiet. It seemed like our little world in my mom's living room had stopped. I felt spent and ready to collapse. I sat on the couch, staring into space, unable to say anything anymore. My mother sat opposite me just making "hm, hm" sounds every few seconds. Frida tried to think of a way to save the situation and us, the two women who were closest to her. I knew that she could understand both of us, but that if she had to "side" with one of us, Frida would probably side with me. That is what I learned from our conversations.

Dialogue with Mother

She later told me that it was the blank look on our mother's face, the incomprehension and disbelief, that sent a shiver down her spine, because deep in her heart she knew that I was right. Frida knew there was something else, something greater than everything else. She knew it because she could feel it when looking at nature's beauty. And she felt it when standing at our grandparents' grave. In a way, Frida told me later that she envied me for this gift of finally knowing where I belonged. At this time, though, Frida was still waiting for that moment, for her epiphany. Nevertheless, Frida continued the conversation and tried to explain my choice with a beautiful example: "Mom, you know, it's like a marriage. Sara has believed in God for a very long time. Now she just made her belief in God official by taking on a religion. She has always been a believer. Now she is a Muslim. Mom, it's like a marriage. You understand? Two people love each other for a long time, and finally they get married. That's when their love is officially recognized. So Sara's belief in God is officially recognized now."

I was astonished at my sister's beautiful explanation. It made perfect sense. Yes, I did get married by becoming a Muslim. Not to any person, but to Islam. I looked at my mother and saw a smile forming on her face as the grey light vanished.

"Yes, I understand," said my mother slowly.

Falling of Fears

Fear is something that has the potential to paralyze a person, especially in these uncertain times. But it is important to understand that Allah is in charge of everything. He oversees the world and all of our life affairs. If we trust Him, we can insha Allah slowly overcome our fears. Suzanna suffered from anxiety but was able to peer through its layers and see the tranquility that Islam promised while she sat in a mosque in Morocco. She converted to Islam in the UK in 2018.

I have always been a fearful person, even when I was young. Maybe because instilling fear was the way my parents tried to educate me and enforce their rules. I was afraid of the dark, of ghosts, of the corner behind the cupboard. I was afraid of strangers because my mom always told me that they might take me away or give me poisoned candy. I was afraid of my teachers and later my boss. My childhood fears followed me into adulthood, where they restricted my life. I was afraid I'd lose my job. I worried that I would not have enough to eat. I worried about being poor during old age when I was 25. I was afraid to go jogging by myself because somebody might rob or rape me, or I might fall and nobody would be there to help me.

Fear controlled me. Then my fears became so bad that I did not even want to leave my home. But even indoors, I was afraid. I knew I had a problem, but I did not know what to do. The problem culminated when my grandmother died, and I began to have panic attacks triggered by the thought of dying myself.

Searching

I went to see a psychologist, but she just wanted to put me on medication to calm me and reduce my fears. It was my best friend who was really there for me, and she came up with a truly crazy suggestion. At least that's what I thought at the time. She invited me to go on vacation with her. She always liked traveling and was constantly searching for something. She invited me to go with her to Morocco. I was afraid, but she assured me that she would never leave me alone. After long discussions, and in the hope of changing my miserable situation, I agreed to join her.

The Call for Prayer

Morocco is really a special country, and I felt the colors, smells, and sounds slowly washing away the upper layer of my deep-rooted fear. We walked through the streets and through the markets. We sat in little cafés drinking tea and just observing life. However, the call for prayer was the most beautiful part of this journey. Every time I heard it, peace would wash over me. I didn't understand the words, but the sound went straight to my heart and for those few moments, I would forget my fears.

One day we were near the entrance of a mosque when the call for prayer was recited. I stood still and closed my eyes. When it was over and I opened my eyes, a lady with a headscarf stood before me and tried to take my hand. All my fears rushed back, and I recoiled. She just smiled at me, and invited me to come with her inside the mosque in broken English. I looked at my friend; she didn't know how to react either. But the lady insisted, so we followed her.

Catching the Peace

Inside the mosque, our new friend invited us to sit and observe the prayer. We listened to the imam reciting the holy verses, and waves upon waves of peace just washed over my fearful heart. Tears flowed from my eyes. I wanted to capture that peace, to keep it. I was afraid it would leave me, and I would be stuck again with all my fears. After the prayer was over, the lady invited us to her house for dinner. Again, I was afraid. What if she offered us poisoned food and wanted to take all our money? The fear was so ingrained in me. But my friend pushed me. She was excited to get to know the real local culture. She assured me that everything would be fine.

Learning About Allah

The Moroccan lady laid before us a beautiful spread. She noticed my hesitation to eat and asked me what was wrong. When I politely replied that everything was ok, she did not seem to believe me and looked at my friend. My friend tried to explain the problem and told her that I had an issue with fear.

The lady smiled and started talking about God. She said that God could take away all fear. She spoke very simply and assured me that we do not need to be afraid because God is in control; we can just leave our affairs to Him. As she spoke about our Creator, her words changed something in my heart.

The Fears Fall

During that holiday in Morocco, I decided in my heart that I wanted God in my life, and I continued learning about Islam when I returned home. The comprehensive understanding of *tawhīd* (the oneness of God) became my focus. The more I learned about Allah ﷻ, the less fear I felt. One day, I felt that I needed to express my gratitude to God. I wanted to submit to Him entirely. *Alhamdulillah*, I recited the *shahāda*. Since then, my anxieties and fears have decreased with every day.

I know that nothing bad will happen to me if Allah ﷻ does not want it to. And every good thing that happens to me is because of Him. This realization removed a heavy burden from me. I understood that we are in this world for a reason. I learned that He provides for me and He takes care of me. What, then, is there to fear?

From Kingdom Hall to the Ka'ba

Although she had been raised in a very restrictive religious home, accepting a gift in return for the Jehovah's Witness pamphlets she left with a Muslim convert was Rebecca's first step toward finding both her own courage and the freedom of Islam. She came to Islam in 2017.

Solid Belief

I have always believed in God. My parents are very pious people, and they raised me to become a disciplined believer. From a very young age, I was aware that my parents did missionary work, and as soon as I was old enough and had acquired the necessary knowledge, I joined them. As a matter of fact, we often went together to knock on people's doors, giving them our small missionary magazines and talking to them. Other times, we would simply stand on the street and distribute flyers, trying to recruit new members to our temple. It was difficult sometimes, especially in winter. But I just followed what my parents told me. They had instilled a fearful obedience in me. I was afraid to be expelled from the temple, to lose my parents and be left alone.

I didn't have any friends, really. I went to a public school in Germany, but my parents did not allow me to bring friends home. I was never allowed to visit them either, or to celebrate their birthdays. The only actual activity I had outside our religious circle was my music class once a week. I don't know why my parents gave permission for me to learn to play the accordion, but I loved it and was grateful for this exception.

First Encounter

When we went knocking, we always checked the names on people's doors or mailboxes. We were instructed not to call on people with Turkish or Arab names. I followed that rule like all the others and never asked questions.

People were often annoyed when we visited and did not want to open their doors. One day, I knocked on a door with a very German name on it and heard shuffling behind the door, but nobody opened. So I knocked again. I heard a woman's voice call for me to please wait a moment. When she opened the door, I was shocked. There stood a Muslim woman, headscarf and all, with a small baby in her arms. She invited us in, but we quickly declined.

A Strange Feeling

I was with my mother, and she signaled me to keep moving, but I could not. The woman with the headscarf was smiling and it seemed like she had a special light around her. I started my sincere pitch about the difficulties and struggles of this life, trying to relate to her situation. She must be very exhausted, I sympathized. I went on about the emptiness many people feel and the meaning of life. She just kept smiling, and I felt something strange in my heart. She, in turn, talked about remembering God all the time. Feeling God, being connected to God. I became confused. My mother

tried to pull me away, and I remembered that we hadn't yet given the woman our literature, so I quickly handed them over.

A Gift in Return

Then something happened that changed my life forever. The woman handed me something in return. I tried to decline it, but she insisted and said: "You gave something to me, so I would like to give you something in return."

I had to take it. It was a copy of the Qur'an. My mother was furious. She took my hand, and we hurried down the stairs.

"We are not supposed to accept anything," she hissed at me.

She wanted to snatch the book from me, but I held it tight and quickly put it in my bag. "You have to throw it away," she continued. But I told her that it was a gift and that we must honor gifts.

I hid the book beneath my mattress and kept it there for a long time. I wasn't brave enough to even touch it. Months later, when I took it out and began to read, I couldn't stop. I just had to read it again and again. I read it like other people read novels. But I didn't know what to do afterward. How to follow the truth I'd discovered.

Brave

Shortly afterwards I met some Muslims on the street who were involved in similar work to Jehovah's Witnesses. I was only out to get some groceries, but I had to stop and talk with them. I told them I had a copy of a translation of the Qur'an, and they were very surprised. They invited me to their Islamic Center. I don't know how I was so brave in that moment, but I joined two of the women and they took me to their small gathering space. The sight of them offering their prayers was the most beautiful thing I had ever seen.

Becoming Muslim

That same night, I held the translation of the Qur'an to my heart and talked with God. I begged Him to guide me, to help me, to protect me. He answered, and I became Muslim *alhamdulillah*.

The hardest part of becoming Muslim was telling my parents. They were so upset that I actually had to leave town. My parents were afraid of being excluded from their community and told everyone I was studying in a different country. It was extremely difficult for them; I'm their only child. Then, after long months of silence, we started talking on the phone. We still have a long way to go, but *alhamdulillah* I've found a wonderful Muslim community that supports me in every possible way.

Prosperity and Purpose

Some of us seem to have everything in life: a nice house, a good car, a well-paying job. From the outside, everything seems perfect. But often this perfection is only superficial. Beneath lurks emptiness and dissatisfaction. If one component of our perfect life breaks away, the house of cards collapses, and we feel close to drowning. Suddenly, the hidden reality of our perfect life reveals itself to us. Anastasia from Mexico seemed to have everything, too. But then her long-term partner broke up with her.

I had everything I needed. A good job, my own apartment. I was "living the dream." I should've been happy, but I felt empty inside. A strange emptiness. I was a Christian, but Christianity was not able to fill that gnawing emptiness. When my long-term relationship did not work out, the emptiness grew into a huge black hole that was threatening to swallow me alive.

Just One Muslim

I'm from a small town in Mexico, about a 90-minute drive from Mexico City. There are no Muslims in my town, and all I knew about Islam was from the media. I believed that Muslims were basically all terrorists and that nothing good could ever come from them. However, I had one Muslim friend who had converted to Islam several years before and moved out of the country.

She was married to a Muslim man and had children, and it was she who stood by me during my most difficult time. She understood my emptiness. She understood the black hole that was threatening to engulf me. And instead of lecturing me about how to get my life back on track like all my other friends and family, she just told me about Allah سُبْحَانَهُۥوَتَعَالَىٰ. She told me about His majesty, His kindness, His mercy. She spent hours and hours of her time chatting with me on the Internet.

Who Is Allah?

Through my friend's selfless efforts, I started to understand that Allah تَبَارَكَوَتَعَالَىٰ is my Creator. This realization was a big relief. It was the first light to fill the scorching black emptiness within me. I wanted to worship Allah عَزَّوَجَلَّ, and I understood that if I did so, He would grant me peace and contentment. Allah جَلَّوَعَلَا would fill the emptiness inside of me. Then one night, He moved my heart. I fell into natural prostration in front of my Creator. I cried. I wept. I poured my heart out to Him. I asked Him to accept me. To accept my life.

A month later, I visited a mosque in Mexico City. I wanted to make my acceptance of Islam official. After I told the brother in the mosque that I wanted to become Muslim, he told me about the requirements for practicing. Praying, wearing a headscarf, and so on. I told him he was crazy and left. But after three days, I returned. I returned with a hijab in hand, said my *shahāda*, and started my journey of learning how to worship Allah.

Learning

I started learning the first *surah* of the Qur'an, al-Fatiha, and a few more short *surah*s. This way, I was able to perform the prayer. I changed my life slowly. I set myself small goals to achieve certain

things in my journey toward Allah. My religious belief changed. I had been Christian and believed that Jesus was God's son. I used to pray to him and ask of him. Now I understood that Jesus was a pious person and a prophet, but Allah ﷻ is One and His essence is indivisible. I stopped drinking alcohol and stopped eating pork.

I also asked Allah to change my job. I worked in an art school and felt uneasy about combining my job with my newfound life with Allah. *Alhamdulillah*, I was able to get a new job a year later. Many people stopped talking to me and many others asked difficult questions. But with every question, my conviction became stronger. I knew that I had made the right choice in becoming Muslim.

It has been over five years now, *alhamdulillah*. I continue my journey of worshipping Allah and working on myself, trying to become a better person every day. I am a wife and mother now, and my family has accepted my new belief and way of life. They are happy that I'm Muslim because they see that being Muslim makes me happy. It's a journey I wouldn't have missed for the world.

What's in a Name?

Mustofa carried a Muslim name, but that was the only Muslim thing about him.

I was born into a family of immigrants and grew up in Chicago. My parents had left their homes and their religion, Islam, in South Asia, where we only returned for short holiday visits. Although my parents didn't practice Islam—my father is an atheist and my mother is agnostic—they followed their South Asian traditions, and so I was given a Muslim name. I grew up in the materialistic world of the big city, went to school and then to college. And it was there that I met other Muslims and was introduced to Islam.

My Muslim Name

I remember my first day at college. I was walking through the hallways where representatives of many different student associations were trying to recruit members from among the newly arrived freshmen. Suddenly, I heard a guy calling out my name. I located him and went over. He asked me if I would like to become a member of the Muslim Student Association. I laughed and said that I wasn't Muslim. He seemed confused. "But you have a Muslim name..." I answered that this was the only Muslim thing about me. I left him standing there and continued on my way. Little did I know that he would become my best friend and first teacher.

Qur'an

Even though I had shrugged it off in the moment, the young man's invitation to join the Muslim Student Association had a lasting impact on me. I looked in my father's huge library for books about Islam. I found a translation of the Qur'an and opened it at random. I did not understand a word of what was written there, although it was in English. I put it back on the shelf and concluded that Islam was not for me. But thoughts about it continued to occupy my mind.

My First Prayer

It wasn't easy to make friends at college, and one day I saw the guy from the Muslim Student Association again. He recognized me right away and even called me by my name. That surprised me. We had a chat, and he seemed like a decent person. So I accepted his invitation to join an informal gathering with other members of the MSA. They were all nice, and many of them were from South Asian backgrounds as well. We discussed philosophy and politics (my favorites at the time). The only thing that was a bit odd was that right in the middle of our conversation, they got up and said they were going to pray. They invited me to join as well. Like their friend, they had assumed I was Muslim because of my name.

It took all my courage to whisper to my new friend Amir that I did not know how to pray. Instead of being shocked, he was very understanding. He whispered that I shouldn't worry, that we would stand in the back where I could just imitate the movements. So that's how I prayed my first prayer as a non-Muslim with a Muslim name. It was Amir's beautiful way of just accepting me the way I was that attracted me to Islam further. He never judged me; he just patiently guided me and tried to answer my many questions. He taught me how to pray, how to read Qur'an, and he introduced me to the works of Imam Al-Ghazali. I could not get enough of his wisdom and spiritual insights. From the depths of my heart, I prayed to Allah to show me the Al-Ghazali of my time.

My First Spiritual Guide

In my final year of college, I met my first spiritual guide and mentor. From him, I learned that there were ways to always remember Allah ﷻ. I learned to draw closer to our most merciful Creator. I learned how to become more pleasing to Him. I learned how to abstain from the things He dislikes—a process that is ongoing and never stops. I learned about Islam from genuine Muslim scholars.

My Family

My parents were surprised when they came to know that I had accepted Islam. I was now a Muslim with a Muslim name. I had many discussions with my father and quiet talks with my mother. After many years, I stopped trying to convince them to embrace Islam. I continue to make *du'a* for them, though. It is the most effective approach. I ask Allah ﵎ to open and change their hearts, and I try to respect and honor them in the most beautiful ways, as Islam teaches.

Islam All Around

Lim sought the answers to several difficult questions before she went from anger to acceptance in 2014.

I grew up in a Chinese family in Malaysia. My parents spoke Cantonese at home and taught us to remember and venerate our Chinese ancestors. We followed different daily and annual rituals than the larger society. Even in our small town, our neighbors and my friends were mostly Muslims. Therefore, I grew up with Islam all around me. I witnessed my Muslim friends performing prayer and fasting during Ramadan. When I was 15 years old, I decided to learn more about the religion that surrounded me. I started asking questions of my Muslim friends. They always welcomed me and tried to answer my questions as best they could. I asked one of my best friends for a copy of the Qur'an. She gave me a Malay translation and, as I started reading it, I became angry. I didn't understand why Allah سُبْحَانَهُ وَتَعَالَى says in His holy book that the disbelievers will not enter Paradise. I was a good person! I didn't do anything wrong! My friend saw my frustration and took me to a proper Islamic scholar. I met with him several times, and he explained the answers to all my questions and confusions.

Am I Not Your Lord?

The scholar explained about Allah and His mercy. He explained how Allah created us and about the covenant Allah made with all the souls He had created. Allah asked all of the souls, "Am I not your Lord?" and all of them answered, "Yes." This fact really made me think, and I continued to learn about Islam.

One day I decided I wanted to be Muslim. I called my best friend and told her about my decision. A few days later, I said my *shahāda* in front of one of the religious officers in the mosque. Both my friend and I were elated.

My Parents

I kept my conversion hidden for some time, but eventually I felt I needed to reveal it to my parents. They were not happy at all. My father told me that I was betraying my Chinese identity, my Chinese tradition and culture, and my Chinese ancestors. The next few months were very difficult for me. My parents tried everything to make me leave Islam. They made sure that they always cooked pork for us to eat, and they encouraged me to drink alcohol with them. In addition, they did not allow me to pray in our home. When I wanted to go out covered with a headscarf, they would prevent me and force me to take it off. It was an enormous challenge.

Leaving Home

I tried to be patient. I tried to be a good daughter. I tried to respect them. I know that Islam teaches respect for parents and treating them with kindness. However, I could not leave my newfound religion. One day, I realized that I had to leave my parents' home. I informed my best friend, and she said that the Muslim community would always take care of me. She picked me up. My heart was heavy, yet light. My eyes cried, yet I smiled. I moved from house to house, staying two months with one friend, and the next two months with another. *Alhamdulillah*, my Muslim community

took good care of me. They helped me financially, and I was able to obtain my first degree.

A Family of My Own

After a few years, I went back to visit my family. They had never replied to my phone calls or messages, and my father did not invite me into the house when I arrived. He just asked me why I had returned. I left without being able to talk to them. I always make *du'a* for them, though. May Allah ﷻ gift them with the guidance He has given me. I have never regretted coming to Islam. I have found the truth; I have recognized my Lord. Praise be to Him! *Alhamdulillah*, I got married and was gifted with a little son. Now I have a family of my own. And *insha Allah*, one day, my parents will open their home to me again. *Ameen.*

A Family Affair

Dedicating one's life to calling others to Islam is an impressive choice. It can include traveling to foreign countries where one doesn't speak the language and sacrificing both wealth and comfort. It takes courage and empathy. Fatima met two such dedicated people in her native village in Laos in 2013.

I grew up in a small village in Laos near the capital of Vientiane. Laos was under communist rule for a long time, and during that time religion wasn't allowed to be practiced openly. Nowadays people there mainly follow Theravada Buddhism, but my family didn't practice much. When I was fifteen, two foreigners brought change to myself and my whole family. Visitors were not unheard of in our village, but these visitors were Black. They drew a lot of attention because we had never had visitors from Africa before. Most people were shy and hesitant to talk to them. My uncle was curious, however, and struck up a conversation with them. He invited them to our home, even though none of us spoke more than a few words of English. The two men were very friendly and smiled a lot.

Where Is Allah?

Our visitors talked about someone called Allah, but no one really understood what they were saying or who Allah was. After dinner, the visitors asked to be allowed to use the washroom. We thought they wanted to take a bath! But they only washed their hands, faces, and feet. Then they took out a small piece of cloth and performed different movements while standing on it. After they were finished, my uncle asked them what they were doing. They explained that they were praying to Allah. All of us were surprised. We didn't see Allah. Where did they put Him, we wondered. Were they carrying Him around in their bag?

No Need for Offerings

Our two visitors explained that Allah is invisible for us in this world. They said that they prayed to Him five times a day, and that they could pray to Him wherever they were.

"Where are your incense and offerings?" my mother asked through my uncle's broken translation. "Does your Allah listen to you if you do not give Him anything?"

With their beautiful smiles, our two visitors answered our questions. Using simple words, they tried to explain the Oneness of Allah ﷻ and the problem with associating partners with Him. No need for offerings, no need for incense smoke, they said. My mother liked that idea. For her, the ritual Buddhist offerings had always formed a burden, both physically and financially. That is why our family had not been very serious about the Buddhist ceremonies.

Even Me?

I tried to follow the conversation closely but was too shy to say or ask anything. There was one important question in my mind that nobody had asked the two men. Would this Allah listen to *me*—a young, uneducated woman? In Laotian culture, it was men who practiced and carried out all the official rituals. Men lived in the monastery. Men were the ones who could obtain a higher form of spirituality. And only men could reach nirvana.

I remember my heart beating violently. My hands began to sweat. I was so nervous. When the conversation stopped, I gathered all my courage and my broken school English to ask the two visitors from the other continent, "Will your Allah even listen to me?"

They looked at me as if they had not noticed me before. Then one of them answered, "Yes, Sister. Allah is there for everybody. We are all the same in front of Him. It doesn't matter whether you are a man or a woman, whether you are rich or poor, white or Black, Asian or African, big or small. Allah is there for everybody. As soon as you call on Him, He will respond and answer you. When you ask Him, He will listen. What makes us different in the eyes of Allah is our piety, our belief in Him. Not our status, not our gender, not our color."

The visitor spoke slowly, and I understood most of it. I was so amazed! I wanted this Allah in my life. I wanted this Allah to listen to me.

A Family Conversion

It took a bit more time, but almost all of my family members accepted Islam. Our two guests visited regularly for a period of about one month. My father, mother, uncle, and older brothers became Muslim. Then they asked me whether I also wanted to accept Islam. I had wanted to since the first time our visitors told us about Allah ﷻ, but I had been too shy to say anything. So when they asked me, I just smiled and nodded my head. I spoke my *shahāda* and started my new life as a Muslim.

Converting to Islam was a big change for my family. We had to change our diet and stop drinking alcohol. Some of our neighbors became suspicious and cut contact with us. But we support one another and *alhamdulillah* the local Lao Muslim community is slowly growing.

I Found God in the Australian Bush

Many of us know the feeling that something is missing in our life. Whether we are born Muslims, converts to Islam, or followers of a different faith. Often what is missing is a spiritual component to our life. We get weary of this ever-evolving, ever-challenging, ever-demanding life. We are longing for spiritual connectedness and tranquility. A time of seclusion can sometimes help us to rediscover what really matters. James converted to Islam in his 60s in 2018 after a long period of just that.

I'm originally from the United States, but I haven't been there for about 30 years. I've spent the last 10 years of my life, my sixth decade, in the Australian bush, where I chose to isolate myself from civilization. I had had enough of everything. I needed a break. A long break. I needed to find myself again and find the purpose of life. Much of my time in the bush was spent in social seclusion, with the bare minimum of worldly things that were necessary to survive. I went to a small town once every two months to get whatever was necessary for my survival. I called my family to check on them. I spent long hours in meditation and contemplation of life.

Thoughts About God

I grew up in a Christian family but left the faith a long time ago. I wanted nothing to do with any religious or social system that sought to enforce its ideology and way of living on me. I had never been a true atheist, but probably would have described myself as agnostic. However, as time went on, my meditation and contemplation had an impact on me. Deep inside, I felt there was this spark of longing for *the* Higher Being, just ready to ignite. I found myself having thoughts about God and His role as Creator and Sustainer. I caught myself talking to Him.

Message From an Old Friend

Then, during one of my visits to "civilization," I decided to check my email account. I hadn't opened it for a long time, but something pushed me to do so. It was full of spam, of course. But one email caught my attention. I knew the name of the sender. It was my old friend from college. He said he'd moved to Malaysia a few years back, and he invited me to a reunion with him and two of our other college friends. I hadn't flown for years, but a few weeks later I was on a plane to Kuala Lumpur.

Seeing a Mosque

My old friend picked me up at the airport and we spent the whole evening talking. He told me he had become a Muslim, which I wasn't really shocked to hear, but I wanted to know more about his choice. The next day he took me to the mosque near his home. It was enormous, with beautiful, plush carpets, and we were the only ones there. The emptiness seemed to provide the perfect space for conversation between a human and their Lord. Strangely, it was that solemn emptiness of the mosque that attracted me most to

Islam. Isolated from the world. Free from civilization—although representing one of the most influential civilizations of the world.

Embracing Islam

I guess God ﷻ just moved my heart; becoming Muslim was the most natural thing to do at that moment. I told my friend that I wanted to embrace Islam. He just smiled at me knowingly. He called two men who were working in the mosque, and we sat down together so I could I recite my *shahāda*.

That was in 2018. Since then, God and Islam have filled my life. I feel like I have finally arrived at the purpose of my existence. It is in prostration to God. In abstaining from food for His sake. In following His commands. Not because any social system tells me to, but because the Lord of the worlds Himself created me for this purpose.

Becoming Muslim was the next natural next step after my solitary life in the Australian bush. I am now able to live in the world without being disturbed by it. I am able to live in seclusion without having to leave civilization. For me, the emptiness of the mosque symbolizes all of that.

Azizah's Choice

Azizah's family experienced an enormous tragedy after she converted to Islam, but her trust in God pushed her to remain strong and determined throughout the trial.

It was February 2005 when I decided to become Muslim, and it was that very day that my mom told me I was no longer her daughter. Her words struck me like a slap in the face.

I had always thought of my mom as all-understanding and all-accepting. Of course, I had expected a "Why?" when I told her of my decision to leave the Catholic church. An "I don't believe you," a "You must be joking," or at worst, a heated argument where I would have to explain myself to her. But I had never imagined in my wildest nightmares anything like disownment.

At first there had just been silence—absolute silence and a freezing coldness on my mom's face. It reminded me of the corpse that had been found in the Alps covered in snow. And then those words were uttered.

"You are no longer my daughter."

The night of those fatal words, I had to pack my few things and leave the house. My younger sister was crying, my older brother said something like, "Everything will be alright." My dad had tears in his eyes. I had never seen him cry, but as much as he wanted to, he could do nothing to help. It was my mother who made these kinds of decisions.

I had no idea where to go. I wasn't the type of woman who changed religions because she got pregnant and had to marry the father of the baby. In that case, I could have just gone to the father of the baby. But I did not have a boyfriend who was Muslim and would marry me. I didn't have *any* boyfriend. My becoming Muslim had had nothing to do with any man. It was my very own personal choice, my innermost wish.

When Sundays at church had begun to leave me unsatisfied, I started reading books about Islam and secretly went to a Muslim couple I knew to learn more. So that night, their house was the only place I could think of to go to.

It was raining heavily when I arrived. The electricity had gone out, as often happened during bad weather in that part of Manado, on the Indonesian island of Sulawesi. When Aisha saw me at the gate, tears running down my cheeks mixing with the rain, she knew what had happened. She came out and enveloped me in a hug even though I was soaking wet. She led me inside and reassured me that Allah سُبْحَانَهُوَتَعَالَى is great and that He would comfort me. It was all His will. I just nodded in silence. I knew that my mother would never take back her words. The stony set of her dark eyes had revealed it.

Three days later, I was on a plane to Yogyakarta. Aisha had arranged a place for me in an Islamic boarding school in Krapyak and paid my fees for the next two years. When I thanked her, she simply said that it was her responsibility to help her new Muslim sister. "And anyway," Aisha smiled, "it's the money we spend on people other than ourselves that will benefit us in the afterlife."

All I could do was promise her that I would always include her in my prayers. Aisha's husband gave me a copy of the Holy Qur'an and reminded me to never stop seeking knowledge. These were

very special, bittersweet moments. Somehow, they helped me to accept my mother's final words. At school, I became fluent in both English and Arabic and started writing religious essays for national and international journals. Then I received a scholarship to Al-Azhar University in Cairo, *alhamdulillah*. This was a big step, and I was extremely excited. However, before undertaking such a long journey, I needed to go back to Manado. I wanted to make one more effort to talk to my mom. Over the past two years I had written her many letters, but never received a reply.

When I arrived at my parents' house, I found it vacant. An empty shell of what had once been the comfort of my childhood, a safe place where my mom consoled me after boys teased me. Where she had waited up for me after midnight mass or welcomed me home on a rainy afternoon with a hot bath already drawn.

Empty. I peered through the uncovered windows and found only dust creeping over the wooden floors. I sat on the staircase and thought about what to do next. I watched the sun set. Then, suddenly, there was a familiar voice. It was my neighbor, the one who had become Muslim because she had fallen in love with a Muslim man. She called me by my old nickname, Lucia. I was so glad to see her. Maybe she knew what had happened to my family and where they'd moved to. She invited me to her house for coffee. As she prepared the strong, bitter coffee of North Sulawesi, she told me of the tragedy that had befallen my family.

"Soon after you left, your mother fell ill with a very strange kind of sickness. Some people in the village said she had been possessed by an evil spirit. From one day to the next, she did not recognize anybody—not your father, not your siblings, not the neighbors. She walked around all day. It seemed she was in search of something. She often got lost and didn't find her way back home, so that your father had to go out and look for her. Many times he found her in the cemetery, sitting in front of a grave with the name Lucia written on it, crying in silence. He always had to drag her home, forcing her to come with him. Then one day, he didn't find her there—or anywhere else. She had just disappeared."

"After months and months of searching, your father finally gave up. He tried finding you instead, but had no clue which way you had gone, where you lived, or where he should begin to look. He finally packed up the family's belongings, took your siblings, and moved on. He couldn't stand the pain of living in a house that was full of memories of you and your mother. He said he was moving back to his hometown to live with his parents in Medan, North Sumatra. He was a broken man, Lucia. The horror of all those endless nights waiting and searching... I could hardly look at him."

I knew it must have been difficult for Dad to go back to his family after he had left them to marry my mom instead of agreeing to the marriage they had arranged for him. I had never been to my dad's hometown. It would take a long time to find him. And Cairo was waiting for me...Cairo and knowledge. I didn't know what to do. Should I search for my family or leave in search of knowledge? I stared into the darkness of the night. The moon was barely visible, and the lights of the village houses looked like faraway planets glowing in the dark. The last sip of coffee left a lingering bitter taste.

Then I remembered the words of Aisha's husband: never stop seeking knowledge. My heart felt tight, my mouth dry. Was I stabbing my father's heart and sending him into the arms of death if I didn't go and search for him? Perhaps. But I couldn't wait any longer. I had to travel to Cairo to study my faith. Burning tears ran down my cheeks and dropped onto the wooden table. It felt like they carved deep lines in my skin. The indescribable numbness that had filled my heart gave way to a new determination that was like a storm blowing away old memories. Yes! I would go to Cairo as I had planned. I fell down in prostration and thanked God for

giving me the strength and the willpower to follow the road that lay ahead of me.

I spent the night at my neighbor's house, and the next morning I left for the airport to catch the first flight back to Yogyakarta. I sobbed in my seat as I took in one last view of my homeland. Somehow, I knew that I would never return.

On arriving in Yogyakarta, I walked slowly out of the airport to catch a bus on the main road to school in Krapyak. Suddenly, I heard someone calling my old name. "Lucia! Lucia!" I was puzzled and didn't react at first, because nobody in Yogyakarta knew me by that name. But the voice came closer and closer until somebody tapped me on the shoulder and called out my name one last time with a deep sigh of relief. "Lucia!" It was then that I recognized my younger sister Maria. I didn't say anything. I just threw my arms around her. I felt tears of joy flowing down my cheeks. I held her tight and felt her heart beating against her chest. I never wanted to let go of her again.

Islam in the USA

The process of conversion is different for every individual. While some people are keen to learn all the rules and regulations and implement them in their life as quickly as possible, others need a broader framework and slower pace to adjust to their new way of life. It's essential to allow each individual to direct their own journey in coming closer to God. Through Michaela's story, we understand that too much information conveyed without the necessary empathy can drive a person away from their search for a spiritual home. Michaela converted to Islam in 2012 in her native country in South America after encountering Islam in the United States.

All I knew about Islam was what I saw in the media: terrorism, oppression of women, and a restricted lifestyle. I come from a Catholic majority country in South America, and very few Muslims live there. Honestly, I had never really thought about Islam or Muslims. However, when I went to the United States to brush up on my English language skills, I came in contact with quite a few Muslims. They were proud to be Muslim and they challenged me and my religious beliefs.

Supplication

I was never really into Catholicism; I was Catholic because of my mom. She taught me everything about the Virgin Mary and how to

make supplication to her. I did not visit church every Sunday, but whenever I had a problem, I would ask the Virgin Mary to please ask God to help me. I never questioned this method of making supplication until one of my Muslim classmates mentioned that Muslims make *du'a* directly to God. That was the first seed of awakening sown into my spiritual consciousness.

No Explanation

Whenever we were free from our English classes, we would try to communicate. Sometimes I spoke in Spanish and my friends spoke in Arabic, but we seemed to understand one another. They often asked me about my religion, and I found that I didn't really have answers for most of their questions. They, on the other hand, seemed well-informed about their religion. I felt bad that I was not able to defend Catholicism and promised myself that I would do my homework once I got home.

Talking Directly to God

However, once I got home, I thought more and more about Islam. I stayed in contact with my Arab friends, and they continued to answer my questions. I started to read about Islam on the Internet, as well, and I started to talk directly to God. It felt strange at first. I felt like a traitor toward the holy virgin. But then I told myself I was just using an expressway to the Receiver of my call. After I began communicating directly with God, everything began to change.

Muslims in My Town

I started looking for Muslims in my hometown. I found two different Islamic centers, but I did not feel welcome at either of them. The first one seemed to cater to one nationality, and the other was too pushy for my taste. When a brother in the second mosque told me all the things I "have to do now" and all the things I "am not allowed to do anymore," I lost interest in knowing more about Islam and Muslims. But I continued talking to God directly, and I felt He was listening.

Not Just Dos and Don'ts

One day, as I was walking through the streets, I noticed a sign that I had never seen before. It read: Qur'an Learning Center. I continued walking past it, but then stopped, turned around, and went inside.

The lady in the center was extremely friendly. She didn't ask me anything nor ask anything of me. She simply invited me for tea and cookies.

The center was blessed with a beautiful, relaxing atmosphere. There was exquisite calligraphy on the walls. Later, my new friend's husband joined us, and I finally told them I was interested in Islam. Instead of regaling me with a list of dos and don'ts, they asked me what I wanted to know. And without being fully aware of what I was saying, I asked them how one could become Muslim.

A Lifelong Journey

The Muslim couple told me that it was easy to become Muslim—that I just had to recite certain words. However, they also reassured me by telling me that becoming Muslim is a process. A lifelong journey of learning and improving oneself. I was surprised at this patient approach to conversion, especially after I had been so pressured at the one mosque, but it attracted me to the faith. A few weeks later, I returned and recited my *shahāda*. My new mentors instructed me to take it easy, to take one step at a time. Islam is supposed to be easy and was not sent to create difficulties for the one accepting it. I took this advice to heart. It has been more than a decade since I embraced Islam, *alhamdulillah*, and I am still taking small steps closer to Allah سُبْحَانَهُ وَتَعَالَى every day.

How Education Brought Me to Islam

The Prophet Muhammad ﷺ was sent as a mercy to all of humanity. Thus, Islam should be there for everybody. As Muslims, we are responsible for the well-being of both our own community and that of others. Providing education free of charge can serve as a strong tool to spread not only knowledge, but goodness and kindness. This is Alina's story.

I'm originally from Laos, a small country in Southeast Asia. *Alhamdulillah*, I had the privilege of finishing high school and continuing my education at university. I longed to attend graduate school, but no opportunities presented themselves. So after graduation I found a good job with an international company. Working for this company provided me with the opportunity to travel to other parts of Asia including Vietnam, Thailand, and China. It was on one of these business trips that I found myself in Malaysia.

The first thing I noticed in Malaysia was that people were not eating when it was time for lunch. I found that strange and asked about it. They told me it was Ramadan and that they were fasting because that was what Allah commanded them to do and they wanted to please Him. After some time, I noticed that they were also not drinking—not even water! I asked again, and they gave me the same explanation. I was astonished. Who was this Allah that people abstained from eating and drinking for His sake?

Who Is Allah?

When I asked my Malaysian colleagues about Allah, they took me to meet a group of European, Asian, and African students they said could answer all my questions. When we walked in, I noticed they were speaking to one another in very fluent English. How and where had they learned it? Where did they study? It was obvious they attended a very high-quality educational institution.

I was informed that they were all students at the International Islamic University. "How can one study there?" I asked. "And is it expensive?" One of the people who was talking to me about Islam told me that if I became Muslim, I could apply for a scholarship. I asked how I could become Muslim, and they told me that I just had to recite a certain phrase, the *shahāda*. I was very excited. Could it be that easy to continue my education? In retrospect, I admit it was probably not the right reason for accepting Islam, but it was my entrance to becoming Muslim.

Becoming Muslim

I spoke my *shahāda* right then and there. I was told that I should cover my head, so I did, and they showed me how to pray. A few days later I applied for a scholarship, and it was granted. I was helped by many people just because I was a new Muslim! I quit my job and continued my education, planning to pursue my PhD. It was all financed by scholarships I was awarded because I was a new Muslim.

Although I had accepted Islam because I wanted an education and a scholarship, that turned out to be only the beginning. During my master's, I started seriously learning about Islam. I learned about *tawhīd*. I learned to read the Qur'an. I became very grateful for the blessings Allah سُبْحَانَهُوَتَعَالَى had bestowed upon me. And with every passing day, I embraced Islam more. I understand now that a free path to education was Allah's way of getting my attention. He knew that was especially important to me.

Free Education

To provide avenues for free education to both Muslims and non-Muslims is extremely important. It should be offered as a service to humanity by our Muslim community. If it was not for education, I may never have become interested in Islam. Quite a few of my friends from Laos followed my example after I told them about this amazing opportunity, and all of them became good, practicing Muslims. Praise be to Allah عَزَّوَجَلَّ. There are many ways to call people to Islam.

Romancing the Faith

In Islam, physical relations between a man and a woman are only permitted within the framework of a legal marriage. This can be a challenge for young Muslim people living in societies where different social behavior is the norm. Suhaila's story beautifully illustrates that the choice to abstain from religiously illicit relations can bring great reward. She converted to Islam over twenty years ago in Germany.

I was raised in a traditional Catholic family in Peru. Sunday service and the Virgin Mary were important parts of my life. I was an obedient child and teenager. I followed what my parents and older family members told me and never questioned my religion. Nevertheless, I enjoyed life.

People in Peru like to celebrate, socialize, and eat. I liked dancing and singing, but I was also keen on becoming successful in life. I finished high school and applied for several scholarships abroad. I was interested in engineering and technical subjects. When I was selected for a scholarship in Germany, I was extremely excited. I bought the only book on learning German in our local bookstore. Three months later, I started my new life in a small university town in the west of Germany.

Muslims Abound

After I arrived in Germany, I attended a German language course for one year. There I met other international students, many of them from Morocco, Syria, and Egypt. This was before 9/11, so there was not much media coverage about Islam. I respected the religion of the Muslim students, and they respected mine. We didn't talk much about religion as a group, but Ahmed was different.

No Dating

During my initial time in Germany, I saw Ahmed quite a lot because we were in the same study group. We met several times a week with two German students to improve our language skills. Ahmed was always in professional mode. At least, that's what I thought. He did not join us when we would go for a drink after our study sessions, and he never tried to ask me out. Actually, it was this last point that impressed me most. And because I liked his calm and respectful demeanor, I plucked up my courage and asked him out one day. He politely declined, and I was puzzled.

The Ideal Muslim Family

Later, I asked Ahmed why he had declined my invitation. He explained that dating was not permissible according to his understanding of Islam. He further explained the importance of a healthy family life, with marriage as the foundation. Dating before marriage can be hurtful to a future marriage, he said, and he believed that it would take away God's blessings. I was stunned. That was a lot to digest. In the coming weeks, I thought through what Ahmed had told me.

In Search of a Happy Family

I had always dreamt of having a happy and blessed family. What I had observed in my immediate surroundings was disheartening, though. Many broken marriages. Cheating spouses. Unhappy families with crying children who did not want to choose between mother and father. Ahmed's attitude impressed me, and what he told me about the position of his faith regarding marriage and family impressed me even more. I began to consider becoming Muslim—not because I had fallen in love with Ahmed, but because I had fallen in love with what he told me about marriage and family in Islam.

My Shahāda

The next time I saw Ahmed in our German class, I told him that I wanted to know more about Islam. Now it was his turn to be surprised. He smiled and told me he had thought I wouldn't want to talk to him anymore. Over the next few weeks, during lunch breaks in the campus cafeteria, he told me about his faith. One day, he asked me whether I was ready to embrace Islam. I had been waiting for this question and said yes. He told me to meet him at the Islamic Center in the afternoon. When I arrived, I found that most of the Muslim students from German class were there, along with some other people I didn't know. Ahmed introduced me to a tall man in a white dress and a white prayer cap, the imam of the Islamic Center. The imam asked me again whether I wanted to become Muslim, and I said yes. Then he read the profession of faith and I spoke after him. *Alhamdulillah.*

A Surprise

But my becoming Muslim was not the only joyful event of the day. After I recited my *shahāda*, some women came over and gave me a beautiful headscarf and some books. We hugged each other, and they helped me put on the scarf. Then, the imam approached us and said that Ahmed wanted to ask me something. In front of all those people, Ahmed asked me to be his wife. I couldn't believe it. Everybody was quiet. Ahmed just smiled at me. It seemed like an eternity. Of course, I said yes. That was over 20 years ago now, and we remain happily married—with three children! Praise be to Allah!

I Felt His Words

Something I really love about Allah ﷻ is that He doesn't just inform us in the Qur'an about miracles of the past, but He continues to work miracles today as well. Some of them are apparent, while others seem less so, but if we open our hearts to Him, we will observe them all around us. This is Anna's story. She converted to Islam in her hometown in Germany.

I was born into an atheist German family. Nobody in my family believed in God. We didn't go to church, we didn't worship anything, we didn't pray. However, from very early childhood, I felt that something big, something amazing, was watching over me. I never really lost this feeling of protection, but it was a long time before it pushed me to search for its source.

Interest in Other Cultures

I liked traveling and I'd always had an interest in other cultures. This led me to major in cultural studies in college. There, I learned that religions are a part of culture, and I grew to see religions as interesting cultural phenomena. I read about Buddhism, Christianity, and different indigenous belief systems. I read part of the Torah, the Bible, and the Qur'an. At the same time, I still had this special feeling inside that somehow connected me with what

I called a Higher Being. One day, I just wanted to know whether this feeling had any basis or not. So I conducted an experiment.

My Experiment with Du'a

I believed this warm feeling of protection must surely have a source. So I asked the source of this feeling to guide me to it. I asked sincerely, but nothing happened. I was disappointed because I wanted a miracle. I had read a lot about people of different beliefs witnessing miracles. Was it all a fraud? Or had they just imagined their miracles? It didn't work for me, that was certain. But I was still left wondering where that feeling came from. Was I imagining it? But it had been with me since childhood. The comforting feeling of being protected by some great Being.

An Inexplicable Experience

A few days later, I sat near my window and looked outside. It was a beautiful spring afternoon. The first buds of light green leaves decorated the trees. The birds sang merrily. The sun was shining. It was perfect. As I sat and observed the beauty, I had these inexplicable feelings and sensations. It was like I could feel the beauty in my whole body. I felt a warm sensation running down my spine. Butterflies were fluttering in my stomach. I had goosebumps on my arms, and the warm feeling of protection seemed to wash in waves through my body and my whole being. I sat still and just reveled in the sensations.

The Answer to My Du'a

I was in awe of what was happening to me, but I managed to stand up and walk to the bookshelf. As if my hand was ordered to, I reached for the Qur'an that was standing next to the Bible and the

Torah. I walked back to my chair, opened the book to a random page, and read the following verse:

> It is Allah Who has sent down the best message—a Book of perfect consistency and repeated lessons—which causes the skin and hearts of those who fear their Lord to tremble, then their skin and hearts soften at the mention of [the mercy of] Allah. That is the guidance of Allah, through which He guides whoever He wills. But whoever Allah leaves to stray will be left with no guide. (Qur'an 39:23)

I was astonished. I was perplexed. This experience, this verse, was the answer to the *du'a* I had made a few days earlier. I read the verse many times. It spoke to me. It explained what I had felt since childhood. It explained the strange experience that had made me get up and open the Qur'an.

Acknowledging My Lord

My *du'a*, the special experience that followed it, and the verse from the Qur'an that explained it were reason enough for me to accept Islam. I didn't know any Muslims at the time. I didn't have Muslim friends or neighbors. That night, I sat down on the floor. I talked to my Lord. I spoke to Allah سُبْحَانَهُ وَتَعَالَى. I thanked Him for His guidance and recited my *shahāda*, with just me and Allah as witnesses. *Alhamdulillah*.

An Exciting Journey

My life since then has been an exciting, interesting, and challenging journey. I've met other sisters on the way, and we've created a support system that especially helps those of us without any family support. I would like to tell everybody who is currently searching for God to listen to your feelings. Listen to your inner voice. Don't listen to what other people tell you. Don't listen to the voices that like to threaten you, insisting you won't be able to handle your new life. You are responsible for your success in this world and in the next life.

From the Nunnery to Islam

Irena Handono is a well-known Indonesian convert. She actively supports converts and spreads the message of Islam. She is the founder of the Irena Center, an Islamic school for new Muslims. She embraced Islam in 1983.

I was raised in a religious Catholic family in Indonesia. For us, being Christian meant that we were different from the majority of Indonesians, who are Muslims. We were rich, educated, and wore fine shoes. The Muslims, so we believed, were poor, uneducated, and always had their flip-flops stolen in front of the mosque. Only much later, during my studies to become a Catholic nun, did I come to question this very shallow view.

Dedicated to God

From a very early age, I received religious instruction. As a teenager, I was active in several of our local churches. I remember always having the aspiration to become a nun. As a Catholic, leaving this worldly life to live in a convent was the most noble thing a young woman could do. I wanted to dedicate my life only to God. So, after I finished high school, I followed His call and enrolled in a Catholic seminary.

Comparative Religion

My parents were very surprised at my decision. I'm the only girl of five siblings, and they had hoped to keep me close to them. But when they saw my determination, they supported my path. My life as an apprentice nun began without difficulties. I was even chosen for special training outside the monastery. I studied comparative religion at the Institute for Philosophical Theology (IPT) and chose to focus on the study of Islam. This was the first time I had ever learned anything about Islam, despite the fact that I had been born in the most populous Muslim country in the world. In the IPT program, I met with the same prejudices about Muslims that were present in my community—that Muslims were poor, uneducated, and uncivilized. For some reason, I couldn't accept that, so I began to do my own research about Islam.

Questions

I had studied in other countries, mostly non-Muslim majority countries, and I found that they all had problems with poverty and education similar to those we faced in Indonesia. India, China, the Philippines, Italy, and many South American countries all struggled with these same issues, though they didn't have large Muslim populations. This intrigued me. I went to my lecturer, presented my facts, and asked for permission to study Islam. My objective was to find the flaws, faults, and weaknesses I knew had to be glaringly obvious in Islam, which I assumed would strengthen my confidence in my own faith.

My First Encounter with the Qur'an

I began by reading the Qur'an, using a copy that had both the Arabic and the translation. Much later I found out that the Qur'an is supposed to be read from right to left, but at that time, I just opened it like any other book and read:

> Say, He is Allah, Who is One. Allah the Eternal Refuge. He neither begets nor is born. Nor is there to Him any equivalent. (Qur'an 112:1-4)

I was amazed by this *surah*. My heart agreed that God is One. That God does not have children, that He is not created, and that nothing is like Him.

Questioning the Trinity

After my first reading of Surah al-Ikhlas, I went to the pastor to ask him about the reality of God. I told him that I had not quite understood the trinity yet. How could God be One and three at the same time? He told me that God is indeed One but has three manifestations or personalities. God the father, God the son, and God the holy spirit. I accepted his explanation, but that night, something pushed me to read Surah al-Ikhlas again: *God is One, He does not beget, nor is He born...*

The next morning, I went again to my lecturer. I told him that I had difficulties understanding the trinity. He went to the board, drew a triangle, and wrote: AB=BC=CA. He explained that the triangle is one, but it has three sides. The same is true for God and the concept of the trinity.

Just Accept

If that is the case, I commented, continuing with his logic of the triangle, one day God might be a rectangle with four sides. The lecturer argued that that was impossible. When I asked why, he became impatient.

"It is just impossible," he said. I continued questioning. There came a point where he said I just had to accept the trinity, even though I didn't understand it.

"Just accept it. Try to digest it. If you question it, you sin."

But I could not digest it. Nor could I accept it. And at night, I went back to the Qur'an and read Surah al-Ikhlas. It pulled my heart toward itself. It was so clear: *God is One. He does not beget, nor is He born. Nothing is like Him.*

Through my own research, I soon came to know that the whole idea of the trinity was man-made. It was in the year 325 CE, during the Council of Nicaea, that the unity of God was split into three. This fact left a deep and painful split in my Catholic identity. Nothing was ever the same.

My Only Refuge

It took another six years before I found the courage to become Muslim and openly proclaim my new faith. When I went to take *shahāda*, the Muslim scholar I had been speaking with asked me if I was prepared to bear the consequences. Converting was easy, he said. But living with the consequences of conversion can be a lifelong challenge. I was prepared. I had to save myself. I had to save my soul. I absolutely could not go back to "just accepting" false dogmas.

The scholar was right. With my conversion, I lost my family. I lost my wealth. I found myself alone. But God was always with me. He was my refuge—my only refuge. As a new Muslim, I knew my responsibilities. I started my five daily prayers, I started fasting in Ramadan, and I covered my head. My life was still dedicated to God, but I was no longer a prisoner to false doctrines and dogmas. I left the monastery but found that as a pious Muslim woman, my whole life is dedicated to God no matter where I am. I don't have to separate myself from the world to be close to Him. *Alhamdulillah*!

Living Religious Freedom, Living Islam

In the present as in the past, there are sometimes vile attempts to erase Islam from a people. Repression, persecution, and cultural and ethnic cleansing have been used to force Muslims to leave their religion. However, the belief and certainty in a person's heart cannot be erased by state control and restrictions. Muslims who live in countries where we are relatively free to practice our belief should remember that this freedom is a sacred blessing. Elmira is originally from Tatarstan, an autonomous republic in Russia. She found Islam while working in Malaysia.

I'm from an ethnic and religious minority group in Russia. Unlike the majority of Russians, who are Orthodox Christians, we Tatars are Muslims. However, during the regime of the Soviet Union, we were prohibited from practicing or displaying our faith. In school, we had to profess atheism. At home, we were too scared to observe any religious rituals. My grandmother still knew how to pray and recite Qur'an, and my mom still knew the prayer movements, but I didn't know anything. All I knew was that we were different. I knew we were "Muslims," but I didn't know what that meant. I was not even allowed to publicly state that I was Muslim.

Freedom

When the Soviet Union collapsed in 1991, I was in my early twenties. The world was suddenly open. We had freedom. And most importantly, we had religious freedom. But taking advantage of it wasn't an instantaneous leap. It took until 1994, the year I began my master's studies, for all bans on Islam to be lifted and a new mosque to finally open in my hometown. I started attending religious classes every Sunday.

A Dream

At first, I could not even recite the *shahāda* by myself, let alone recite any prayers. Then one night I had a strange dream. In my dream, I saw a beautiful building with a huge, ancient-looking door. I opened the door and found stairs covered with green carpet. Something made me walk up the stairs. I found myself in the midst of a magnificent hall and performed prayer there. I felt so peaceful and pleased when I woke up in the morning. After a few days, I had the same dream again, and after a week, the same dream came again. In my dream, I performed the prayer. Then one night I heard a firm male voice telling me: "Pray, pray, pray."

Learning and Living Islam

I woke up feeling scared, my entire body shaking. I so wanted to pray. I took my notes from Sunday school and repeated the verses from the Qur'an that are necessary for prayer, repeating this process four more times that day. I started praying regularly beginning that morning. I will never forget the feeling of joy and release when I made my first *sajdah*. I had never had such a feeling.

Finding a Place to Pray

Praying five times a day wasn't difficult, but finding a place to do it was. At that time, the mosques in Kazan were still few and far between. Some resorted to praying in dirty storerooms at the university, hiding from security, or even sitting down on public transport. But the most difficult part was finding the correct *qibla*. At home, my parents still knew the direction of Mecca, but in other places, it was often a process of trial and error to find the right direction for prayer.

Another Blessed Dream

When I started praying it was winter, and the sun was often covered by clouds. This made it extra difficult to locate the *qibla*. But I needed to know the right direction to face my Creator, especially when I moved to a dorm. There were no apps or gadgets at that time, so I just made *du'a* that Allah would help me with this tricky task. And *alhamdulillah*, He sent me another blessed dream.

I saw myself praying in my dorm room, which was full of light and peace. Then, an aged but very handsome man in white cloth came to me, directed me to one side, and said, "My daughter, the *qibla* is here."

When I woke up, I was very happy. From that day onwards, I always faced that direction during prayer. Later, I came to learn that this was indeed the right direction. Praise be to our most merciful Lord.

Kindness

Contrary to its twisted portrayal in mainstream media, Islam is a religion of inclusion and kindness. As Muslims, we are taught to be kind, to serve our neighbors, and to give in charity. When Katja learned how gentle and inclusive Islam teaches us to be, she made it her religion for life.

When I was in my early twenties, I was looking for the path to take in my life. I'm originally from Russia but came to Germany when I was a child. My grandmother is very religious, so I had studied the Bible. I researched Buddhism as well, looking for the right path. But then, I learned about Islam, and I was amazed at what it teaches about kindness and tolerance. Kindness to our neighbors. Kindness to the orphan. And what was really surprising: kindness to the nonbeliever and even the enemy! In 2013, I took my *shahāda*. And then my life turned upside down.

Fear and Prejudice

I began to cover my head and wear long dresses. My family was not at all happy with my choice; they were filled with fear. However, I suspected that all they needed was information and explanation. So I took the time to sit down with my family and explain my choice. I always tried to be friendly and open and, *alhamdulillah*, with time, they accepted my decision.

The Differences Confused Me

When I first converted to Islam, I was often worried about not doing things correctly. I was confused about the differences in prayer movements. People in the mosque prayed in slightly different ways, and everybody claimed their way was correct. There were also various ways to recite Qur'an and many confusing cultural practices. I was at a loss and realized I needed to study Islam more deeply.

Diversity as a Blessing

After some years, I was blessed to meet a wonderful teacher. She explained that slight differences in understanding and practice of Islam are normal. In fact, they're a blessing. We each choose one way that we will follow. So I eventually learned to recite Qur'an in one of the 10 traditional recitation styles. I learned the prayer of one *madhab* (school of thought). And I know when I see others praying differently that they are following a different *madhab* and that's great.

The Spirit of Learning

The spirit of learning is also something I appreciate about Islam. Our faith is not dogmatic but rather a religion that wants us to understand. We are encouraged to ask questions and follow an open process of getting to know our Creator. One of the advantages of continuously seeking knowledge is that our confidence grows. Somehow, after my conversion, I often felt like a little child. I was new. I didn't know anything, and everybody I met wanted to teach me something. This impacted my self-confidence and self-worth. But with every new bit of knowledge and every new understanding, my self-confidence grew. This doesn't mean I felt I was better than other people, but that I began to feel stronger in myself, and

this was a huge blessing on my journey. Basically, I continue the process of converting because every day I learn something new.

No Difference Between the Genders

In Islam, everybody has the potential to become knowledgeable. Any man or any woman can become a religious scholar. And any man or any woman has the potential to become a close, intimate friend of Allah عَزَّوَجَلَّ. Praise be to Him. From the spiritual perspective, all humans are equal. And this is one of the most powerful teachings of Islam. What differentiates us from one another is not any outer attribute, but rather our love for and obedience to Him.

Inspired by Islam Since Childhood

Converting to Islam is not a one-off event but a lifelong process of searching for and learning about the Truth. It often starts long before one actually embraces the faith, with a childlike inquisitiveness about foreign ritual practices or an interest in religion or spirituality that stems from an emptiness inside. Peter Schütt, born in 1939, is a German journalist, author, and political activist. He found his religious home in an Islamic Center in Hamburg, Germany. His story illustrates the process of conversion in an inspiring way.

I spent more than half my life searching for the true religion. I was born into a Lutheran family and when I was 19, I converted to Catholicism. I needed more spirituality and wanted to get away from the narrowness of my Lutheran home. This was actually the only drastic shift in my religious life. Thirty years later, I officially announced my conversion to Islam, but embracing Islam was not a drastic shift. Rather, it was the final result of my search to gain spiritual insight and realization.

I was fascinated with Islam from an early age. I grew up in a small village in post-war Germany that belonged to the British occupation zone. Some of the soldiers were from British India, and they were Muslims. They were very kind to us children, giving us dates and figs. I was intrigued by their prayer movements, and this memory of observing the Islamic ritual prayer stayed with me.

Stories About Pilgrimage

It was in a venerable old church near my home village that I learned about well-known Germans who were interested in Islam. The pastor of the church told me about these famous Germans who had studied Islam. Carsten Niebuhr, for example, was called the first German hajji by the famous German poet, Goethe. These stories filled my heart with excitement and curiosity. I wondered about this special place called Mecca and why people traveled from far and wide to reach there.

Theology of Liberation

During my studies at the university, I again encountered Islam. I especially focused on the art and culture of the East. In the dorms, I lived in the same hall with Muslim students from Iran, Egypt, and Nigeria. We spent nights discussing religion and belief, and we organized interreligious dialogue forums on campus. During that time, I saw Islam as a theology of liberation for the people of the "third world." My African Muslim friends on campus were among those who inspired me to bring down the memorial monument of Herrmann von Wissmann, a German colonial butcher who massacred people in East Africa. I was politically active and took part in the student revolt.

My Mosque

In 1991, I finally took my *shahāda* with the guidance of my teacher Mehdi Razvi. The Islamic Center located near the Alster river in Hamburg became *my* mosque. It is a modern mosque—not just a place of worship but a place for many different activities.

Interreligious dialogues and discussions are important regular events at the center. Engaging speakers from all over the world come to talk about Islam.

Patience

It took more than half of my life for me to finally arrive at Islam. However, that is not the end point. One's *shahāda* is the beginning of a continuing journey. Becoming a true believer with your entire heart and soul is a lifelong learning process. You have to realign your intentions every day and deepen your knowledge about Islam every day. It takes patience and perseverance. For example, it was in 1967 that my teacher began teaching the interpretation of the Qur'an in our Islamic center. His successor has still not finished the whole Qur'an. Understanding requires time. Just as I did not become a Muslim overnight, but rather treaded a long road of discovery. And *insha Allah*, if God wills, I will continue to draw closer to the truth with every day of my life.

From Fame to Faith

For some of us, life is good. We have plenty, enjoy it, and don't feel the need to look more closely at ourselves. Sometimes, though, Allah ﷾ has better plans for us. He knows our full potential and will push us in unimaginable ways to become the best possible version of ourselves. Maik Jahnke was a famous hip-hop star in Germany before he had a bad car accident that changed his life in many ways and ultimately brought him to Islam.

I grew up in a normal German family. I went to school, learned a profession, and then worked. But all along, music was my true passion. As soon as I was earning my own money, I bought musical equipment. I wrote my own songs and composed my own music. I slowly worked my way up in the music business. My music partner and I were able to get one contract, then a second. Eventually, we scored with one of the biggest record labels in Germany. We played everywhere, including MTV. Life was good. Money was good. Then one morning, I had a horrible car accident.

Nothing Was the Same

After my car accident, I became very thoughtful. I wondered about this life. The essence of this life. The reason for this life. Why was I here? What was this life for? At night, I stepped out onto my balcony and looked up in the sky. What was the purpose of all this? What was my role in it all?

Talking to God

I had always believed in God, but I never had much to do with any official religion. During the time after my accident, my writings changed. The object of my writings was God. I wrote about Him, I wrote to Him, I was looking for Him. I found consolation in writing, but the questions remained.

A Wake-Up Dream

One night, I had an amazing dream. I was in a different time. There were no cars or airplanes. I stood in a desert outside the walls of a town. I could see camels in a caravan walking toward the city. And next to me was a handsome man with black hair and a beard. He had a stick in his hand. He used it to write something in the sand. Then he looked up at me. He asked me whether I understood what he was writing. I did not. Then I woke up, shaken. I cried for two hours.

Several of my friends interpreted this dream as being about Islam. Seeing me in a state of searching and questioning my existence, they told me to follow that dream. And that is what I did. I started reading about Islam. Then I just went to the city of Aachen, where we have a big Islamic Center, and recited my *shahāda*.

New Path

After I recited my *shahāda*, I started to learn what it meant to be a Muslim. I learned the five daily prayers. I started reading Qur'an. I found answers to my questions about existence and the true purpose of this life. I found peace and contentment in worshipping God. I found a new community, and I certainly became a better person. Before becoming Muslim, I hadn't liked foreigners much, but learning about the diversity of the Muslim community allowed

me to give up every bit of racism still left inside. And along with it, I gave up my life in show business.

Visiting God's House

Performing Hajj and Umrah were amazing experiences for me. Witnessing this beautiful, diverse community of people, all worshipping God, was astonishing. Learning and pondering upon the history of humanity from Prophet Adam to Prophet Ibrahim, father of the three main world religions, and our beloved Prophet Muhammad ﷺ was truly humbling. I came home as a new person.

For those who are still searching: look at the sky. Look at this amazing creation. Look how perfectly everything is created. Listen to your heart, and you will find God. You will find Islam. You will find the purpose in this life. And you will find the peace you need and contentment you are looking for, *insha Allah*.

I Went to Help Refugees, but They Helped Me

Helping other people brings many blessings—some are expected, and some come as a surprise. Max experienced both kinds when he worked as a volunteer during the 2015 refugee crisis in his small hometown in Germany. Max is now in his twenties.

I was an ordinary teenager: parties, girls, alcohol. I had fun. But there was also this other side of me. I was adopted as a baby, and ever since I began to understand what that meant, I'd felt an empty space inside. I wondered where I had really come from. Maybe it was this disconnect from my own origin that propelled me to jump in and help when the first refugees from Syria and other countries arrived in our small town.

Knock, Knock

In September 2015, I went to meet the refugees for the first time. I just knocked on the door of the refugee center near me and said I was there to help. From then on, I could be found there almost every day. I made the beds, cleaned the floors, and accompanied refugees to the doctor. I played with the kids. In the evening, instead of going home, I relaxed with them. We drank tea together and I listened to their stories. Stories of grief. Stories about the war. Stories of leaving one's homeland. Of missing family. We also talked about religion and beliefs.

Why Don't You Have a God?

One day, a female teacher from Lebanon said to me, "You help so much. You do so much good. Why don't you have a God?" Why *did* I not have a God? I turned this question over and over, but I didn't have an answer. I had never really had a connection to the Christian idea of God. But beginning from that evening, I listened carefully when my refugee friends talked about Islam. I observed them praying and asked myself, *How would it be to live with Allah, to live as a Muslim?*

The Leap

One morning in spring of 2016, I woke up and thought, *I will convert to Islam now.* It was a Friday. I sat down in front of the computer and googled how one could become Muslim. Then I dressed, took my bike, and went to the small mosque in our town. I went straight to the imam, introduced myself, and informed him that I wanted to become Muslim. I had already chosen a Muslim name: Yaser, the helper.

Backlash

When my mother found out I had become Muslim, she was shocked. She thought I would become "one of those radicals." She was horribly afraid of losing me. For the first two weeks after my conversion, she cooked only pork. I didn't eat it. When I asked her about it later, she said she hadn't done it on purpose. She was having difficulties adjusting to the new circumstances so quickly. I was only 17 years old and had become a Muslim of all things. During those first few months after my conversion, we often ended up in heated discussions and arguments. But it has improved now, *alhamdulillah*. My mother found that I remained the same person I had been before and gradually her fear of losing me receded. She knows that Islam is important to me, and she respects my new way of life.

Some Friends

When I told my friends about my decision, I was met with silence. I could no longer drink and party with them, and all of them slowly left my life. I wasn't sad about it. That's life. We took different paths. I found my way in Islam, in prayer, and in following Allah's commands. I love going to the mosque. I'm studying Arabic and learning to read the Qur'an. I'm also succeeding in my second year of learning a profession. It's my third attempt, and the stability of my life as a Muslim is the blessing that has allowed me to succeed.

Losing it All

Many people coming to Islam experience rejection from their families. Some are disowned and have no place to go. The Muslim community becomes their family, and the mosque becomes their home. Our beloved Prophet Muhammad ﷺ reminded us that the Muslim community is like one body. If one part of it aches, the whole body feels it. Therefore, we strive to ease the pain of each part of our community the best we can. This is Abdullah's story. He is from Indonesia and embraced Islam in early 2019.

I grew up in a strict Christian family in Indonesia. Although my family lives in a Muslim-majority country, we have always held tightly to our Christian faith and identity. We had mostly Christian friends, and my father dealt almost exclusively with Christian business partners. We went to church regularly, and I went to a Christian school. Later, I spent two years acquiring deep knowledge of the Christian faith at a seminary.

Quiet Step

However, from an early age, I was also taught about Islam. Only later did I realize that this was to enable us to do missionary work. Nevertheless, looking back, the first step in my conversion was actually found in one of the books my father gave me. It was about the Crusades, and it was meant to strengthen my spirit for doing missionary work in different parts of Indonesia. I liked the book very much, especially the parts about the great Muslim warrior, Salahuddin al-Ayyubi.

Tolerance and Chivalry

Salahuddin was totally different from the Christian crusaders, who killed left and right, men and women, old and young. I was amazed by this Muslim commander who not only tolerated but respected religious minorities and even gave them rights after his army took over their territory. I was in my early teens during this time, and the chivalry that Salahuddin al-Ayyubi displayed toward religious minorities impressed me tremendously. He didn't force anybody to accept Islam. People under his rule were free to practice their religion peacefully. He became my secret hero.

This story stayed with me, and whenever I felt that we, as Christians, were not being tolerant, I remembered Salahuddin. In my late teens, I started reading more about Islam. I visited Muslim websites. I genuinely wanted to know about the true message of Islam. I started to have online Muslim friends. They were exceedingly kind and answered my questions as well as they could.

Outside My Circle

I started working in my father's construction company. I worked well and he trusted me, and so the day came when I was given my first independent contract in another city. Being outside my familiar circle was great. I finally had a chance to connect with people who were not close Christian family or friends. Whenever I went out for lunch or dinner, I would talk with the people who sold the food or other customers. I was met with friendliness and openness. One day I met a guy named Faisal, who became one of my best friends. He was a Muslim, was also new to the city, and was

full of love and passion for his religion. One day, I just followed him to a mosque and announced my *shahāda*.

Soaring and Crashing

I felt like a new person. I felt alive. I loved the mosque. I loved the prayer. And because I was so happy and so convinced, I eagerly told my father when he came to check on the construction project.

In a matter of seconds, my whole life changed.

I cannot say what he said or did, because he is my father and I still want to respect and honor him. But in a matter of seconds, I lost everything. I lost my father. I lost my family. I lost my money. I lost my work. I lost all my business contacts and friends. *Alhamdulillah*, I was able to move in with Faisal, and he helped me out over those first few months, both spiritually and financially.

Paying it Forward

That was almost one year ago. Together with my brothers in faith from the mosque, I was able to get back on my feet quickly. We are now trying to set up our own business but have bigger goals as well. I have come to understand that many Indonesian Muslim converts share similar experiences to mine, and we want to establish a support network that will be there for them during this transition, just like Faisal and the brothers were there for me.

I Used to Believe in a New Prophet, Then I Found Islam

The human need for spiritual well-being and the desire to worship Allah the right way is what pushes many people to search for the Divine. Alhamdulillah, He has provided us with concrete and uplifting instructions on how to both care for our souls and worship Him. Following these instructions promises to bring salvation for the searching soul. This is Nasima's story. She converted after a long search to understand how God wants to be worshipped.

I was born in Iran. My father was Muslim and my mother of Jewish descent; however, they had both converted to the Baha'i faith. Baha'i is a relatively new monotheistic religion that claims there were prophets after Prophet Muhammad ﷺ. I was raised as a Baha'i, and we had a good life. But when the Iranian revolution took place in 1978, we had to flee the country. I went to the Netherlands and started my studies there. My mother and father ended up in Germany.

Freedom and Confusion

My father was from a very religious Muslim family. He could even trace his lineage back to the Prophet Muhammad ﷺ. But he was totally convinced of his new faith. It came to liberate people, he said. We believed in God and we worshipped Him, but this worship did not bring peace to my heart.

I saw how different our form of worship was from my Muslim neighbors and friends. My father explained that our way of worship was in step with the mental and emotional development of humanity, but honestly, when I was young, the different ways of worshipping God in the Baha'i faith confused me. Even my parents had different ways of worshipping. My mother had her own way, and my father had his. They told me to follow whatever way I liked. But instead of liberating me, as my father thought, this confused me. Many times, I just didn't worship at all.

Art Is Life

When we fled Iran, I went to the Netherlands and studied art. I was separated from my family and didn't meet any other Baha'is. I had books about my Baha'i faith but scarcely read them. I immersed myself in my art studies and, in a way, art became my religion. When somebody asked me about my faith, I would loyally reply, "Baha'i," but I didn't find any contentment in that answer. Art became my life, but it also added to my confusion and restlessness. I would be in my studio for days on end…working, painting, but never sleeping. I lived alone in my world of colors and shapes, but I was lonely. I felt that nobody understood me. Because of financial difficulties, I almost never went to visit my family, and they didn't visit me either. The years flew by. I was 30 and had done nothing in life except paint. I took out my old Baha'i books and tried to find some peace in practicing the faith. But again, the loose definitions of worship confused me. I already had freedom and liberty in my art. What I needed was clarity and structure.

Travel

My professor at the art college seemed to know that something was wrong. He sensed that I had been procrastinating on my final project because I didn't really want to finish. He advised me to go traveling. I didn't have the money for globe-trotting, so I applied for a scholarship to study and travel in Indonesia for one year. I left everything as it was, very sure of my return. In Indonesia, I visited different islands but stayed mainly in Bali and Java. I met many Indonesian artists, and their attitude toward life impressed me. They seemed to be always positive, even in difficult situations. I became close with one young artist. When he asked me to be his wife, I asked my father and he agreed.

The Last and Final Prophet

My husband is Muslim. When he asked me about my religion, I told him I was a Baha'i. He had never heard of the faith, so I explained that it was a new monotheistic religion after Islam, and that we also believed in the One and only God. He explained that there is no true religion after Islam because the Prophet Muhammad ﷺ was the last and final messenger. Of course, I did not believe him, but I needed to convert on paper in order to get married. So I said the *shahāda* without intending to really become Muslim.

Afraid

We lived together for many years. Sometimes I prayed together with my husband the Muslim way. I felt good during these prayers. I felt at peace. But I was still afraid of leaving my parents' religion.

Then, one day, I met a Muslim scholar who was able to explain all the misconceptions of the Baha'i faith. It all made so much sense. My father had passed away by then, and my mother was far away. I was in my mid-forties and really worried about my mental and spiritual well-being. I needed concrete guidance. And I needed to worship God the way He wants to be worshipped.

My True Shahāda

After almost fifteen years of being married, I took my *shahāda* again—this time to truly become Muslim. I needed spiritual stability in my life. I needed a clear way to express my love for God. Islam provides that. And I was convinced that our beloved Prophet Muhammad ﷺ was truly God's last and final messenger.

Monotheism for Life

During my time working with converts, I've seen that the question of "What will my family say if I become Muslim?" causes more people to hesitate in taking their shahāda than any spiritual concern. Some converts begin their new faith journey without their family's knowledge; others are open with their Islam from the first moment. Some families are open and kind, while others struggle to accept the change and, as we have seen, some outright disown their new convert. But always, the lesson for us is that we must always be ready to support the new Muslims around us in whatever way they need. This is Aron's story. He is from a Jewish family in New York City and converted to Islam after his student exchange year in Indonesia.

I grew up Jewish in New York City. My forefathers came from what is known today as Poland. They left their home after 1795, when the increasingly antisemitic Russian Empire controlled parts of Poland. My family aren't Orthodox Jews, but Judaism did play a significant role in our life and was an important marker of our identity. We followed the traditional rituals and celebrations while engaging with the society around us.

Music Brought Me to Indonesia

At an early age, I developed a passion for music. By the time I was in my teens, I was deep into both experimental and traditional music and instruments from different parts of the world. I would use the different sounds and include them in my own compositions. One day, a friend told me that you could major in ethnomusicology in Indonesia. I was determined to travel there and enroll in an art institute that offered such a degree.

Undercover

When I arrived in Indonesia and enrolled at the institute, I didn't tell anybody that I was Jewish. In Indonesia, you have to state your religion, so I just stated that I was Buddhist. That was the easiest choice at the time. I was worried that people would show hostility towards me if they knew I was Jewish. And since I didn't practice my religion to a great extent, I didn't mind claiming to be from another tradition. To be honest, during that time in the early 2000s, it was kind of hip to claim that one was Buddhist. Indonesians viewed "new Western Buddhists" as exotic and didn't ask uncomfortable questions.

Music First

I lived in Indonesia for more than two years. During that time, I participated in many music projects and tried to stay out of religious discussions as much as possible. I concentrated on my music, and my Jewish religious traditions became very distant. I was away from my family, away from my Jewish community, and away from all the traditional celebrations. Islam seemed like this local religion that was just not for me. And frankly, I thought practicing Muslims spent too much of their time praying rather than doing really important things.

Gamelan and Islam

Then one day I joined a traditional gamelan performance. The gamelan is a traditional Javanese percussion instrument made from metal. Next to me sat an old man, and he began talking to me. It was in the middle of my second year, and my Indonesian had become quite good. He explained the connection between the gamelan and Islam. He told me about an ancient royal gamelan ensemble whose only purpose was to commemorate the birth of the Prophet Muhammad ﷺ. The gamelan *sekaten* is bigger than all the other gamelans and is only used once a year. The old man explained that the playing of this gamelan is supposed to represent continuous praises for the Prophet Muhammad ﷺ. This story impressed me because I had never thought about the spiritual aspect of music. His explanations made a lasting impact on me.

Reading About Islam

I continued composing experimental music, and my gamelan recordings became an important part of it. I started reading more about the spiritual aspects of Islam and especially the so-called Islamic mysticism of Indonesia. I had seen Islam as a dry, strict religion that only focused on halal and haram. Reading about Islam in Indonesia, however, I learned that my perception was far from reality. I began to understand that Islam was a lived religion and that it was full of the spirituality I wanted in my life. The more I read, the more interested I became. I also read about Islam in other places and was fascinated by its richness.

Following My Heart

I was interested in embracing Islam and becoming Muslim, but I worried about my family. What would they say? A Jew becoming

Muslim? I didn't want to lose them. Eventually though, I followed my heart. I said my *shahāda* in a small Muslim community center in New York City. I started praying and joined their regular *dhikr* circle. The rhythmic remembrance of Allah is wonderful, like spiritual music that soothes the heart and calms the mind.

Telling My Family

I didn't tell my family about my conversion for a long time. Since I didn't live with them anymore, it was quite easy to keep it hidden. I tried to get around religious celebrations and Jewish community gatherings, but eventually they became suspicious. When I told them, they were just quiet for what seemed like forever. Then my mother asked me if I was happy, and I said "Yes!"

But my father made a request: "Can you please wait to make it public? I mean, nowadays people have bad opinions about Muslims. I don't want our friends to think negatively about you or us."

I complied with my father's request, and I still do. We just don't talk about religion. I only very occasionally join Jewish community gatherings. Otherwise, I keep a low profile. This arrangement has been working well for all of us. It allows me to practice my faith and still be part of my family.

I Saw Angels

Allah ﷾ uses diverse ways to attract people to Islam. People are awed by different factors, and Allah knows what will work for any given person and what won't do. Each way is special and uniquely designed by Allah, but some stories seem more spectacular than others. The following story is inspired by Muhammad Cheng's experiences. He converted to Islam in 2005, after the devastating tsunami hit his hometown of Aceh, Indonesia.

Although I was born in Indonesia, I'm not Indonesian. I'm of Chinese descent. Three generations ago, my family came to Aceh—in a very Islamic part of present-day Indonesia—for trade. The rulers were just, and the people were as well, so they stayed. My family kept our Chinese traditions of venerating and worshipping our ancestors, and I did the same. Before I opened my shop each morning, I would give offerings on the altar of our ancestors. During the day, I repeated the offering of incense several times. My shop was very close to the Grand Mosque, and I could hear the call to prayer every day, but it never occurred to me to become Muslim. Never until that fatal morning.

Just Like Any Other Morning?

I was just about to open my shop near the Grand Mosque of Banda Aceh on December 26, 2004. It was a regular morning. Nice weather. Nothing out of the ordinary. At least, it seemed so. But the birds had stopped singing...that was strange. And the cats that usually waited in front of my shop for some leftover food were suspiciously absent. I didn't pay much attention to these oddities, but all of a sudden there was a strong rumbling and a loud sound. I ran outside. *It must have been an earthquake*, I thought. Other people emerged from their shops as well, but after a few minutes of quiet, we all returned to work.

The Sea Is Coming

Shortly thereafter, people came running and screaming down the street. "Water! The sea is coming. Water!"

I was so confused. Although I understood the words, I couldn't fathom what they meant. I went outside again. People were hysterical, running toward the mosque. Screaming. Shouting. And then I saw the water racing toward us. I ran to get my incense; I wanted to ask my ancestors for help, but the water was rushing, gushing down the street and toward the mosque, just behind the frightened, fleeing people. Terrified, I ran upstairs. I looked out from my small balcony. An unbelievable torrent of water flooded the street—and more was surging in every second.

Was I Crazy?

As I turned toward the Grand Mosque I marveled at what I saw. Tall men dressed in white clothes were standing in front of it, making movements like policemen directing traffic. *And the water was following their directions.* The water split a few meters in front of the mosque and flowed past it on either side.

The water kept coming. The full force of the sea shoved its way into the city and toward the mosque. But the men dressed in white did not run away like everyone else. Hundreds and hundreds of people rushed toward the mosque, running for their lives. Some fell, and the water took them. I saw all this from my balcony. The water rose higher and flowed faster. But it never entered the mosque, and the people inside were safe. Then, all of a sudden, more men dressed in white appeared and they *lifted up the mosque.* Yes! They lifted the whole mosque up just above the ground, and water gushed underneath. I was totally stunned.

Telling

If somebody had told me the story of what I saw, I would never have believed him. Never! But I saw it with my own eyes. I was wide awake. *God is protecting this mosque,* I said to myself again and again. Weeks after the disaster, I pushed myself to tell the Muslim shopkeeper next door what I had seen. He advised me to meet the *ustadh* in the mosque. Although I had lived next to it my whole life, this would be the first time I would enter the mosque compound.

The *ustadh* recognized me from afar and came outside to greet me. "Good morning. Can I help you, Uncle?" he greeted me politely.

He listened quietly to my story, and tears flowed from his eyes. After I finished, we just hugged. It was this natural hug that people exchange because they have gone through the same horrific experience. The *ustadh* said: "Uncle, what you saw were God's angels following God's command. God decreed that His mosque would not be destroyed. Maybe God allowed you to see them in order to bring you closer to Him— because He loves you, because

He sees you are a kind man. He wants to give you happiness in this world and Paradise in the next. Would you like to become Muslim, Uncle?"

Pondering

I was shocked at the *ustadh*'s question. It confused me. How could I, a Chinese man, become Muslim? We Chinese people have our own traditions, rituals, and beliefs. I thanked the *ustadh* and left. I went back to my shop, kept the doors closed for the day, and just sat quietly in the corner. Again and again, I saw before my eyes the scenes of the day the tsunami hit. The men dressed in white clothes directing the water. Lifting up the mosque. God's angels doing His work. And I was allowed to witness it. I did not open my shop the next day or the next. I just sat inside and pondered.

A Bright Light

On the third day, someone knocked on the door. It was the *ustadh* of the mosque looking for me. He was worried because my shop had been closed for three days—something that had never happened before. "I was thinking, *ustadh*," I told him. "I think you were right. God gave me a sign. A huge sign. I should not be a fool now and just forget about it. Can you tell me how to become Muslim?" "It is very easy," the *ustadh* said. "You just need to recite these words."

And he showed me a piece of paper. I recited the words, and it was as if a bright light filled my shop. After that, the *ustadh* came every day to teach me about Islam. He showed me how to pray and how to read Qur'an. Joining the prayer in the Grand Mosque was and is one of the most beautiful things in my life. *Alhamdulillah*.

I Ran Toward the Mosque

Friendship and caring for a person can transcend religious, ethnic, and other boundaries. And sometimes the result of our caring is the opening of someone's heart. Ahmed is originally from East Timor, a small country in Southeast Asia that gained its independence from Indonesia in 2002. He embraced Islam over twenty years ago.

I was born and raised in East Timor, a small island east of Indonesia. The island had been a Portuguese colony, so most people, including my family, followed the colonizers' Catholic faith. The economic situation there has always been rather unstable, and I left home early to earn a livelihood. I lived in Jakarta, the Indonesian capital, but one day, I received a good offer to work in a town in South Sumatra.

My Friend Prayed for Me

I went to South Sumatra and started working there. I shared a room with a Muslim coworker, and we got along well. Indonesians usually don't have a problem with people of other faiths, and my roommate and I were no exception. He was a kind person, and we became fast friends. Sometimes, he would perform his prayer in the room, and afterward he would make *du'a*, mentioning my name. He also regularly read the Qur'anic chapter called Yasin.

After reading Yasin, he would also mention my name. He did this every time, and I became curious to know why he always mentioned my name after his prayer.

"You are my friend and fellow human. I want the best for you, so I pray for you." I was touched by his explanation, and it opened my heart to try and learn about Islam.

Yasin

When my roommate wasn't home, I developed a habit of taking out his little *Yasin* booklet and reading the transliteration in Latin script. Afterward, I would make supplication as I had learned in Sunday school as a child in East Timor.

A Serious Illness

One day I became seriously ill. I had a high fever and felt very weak. I could barely walk from my room to sit on our small terrace. That evening, my friend went to pray Maghrib in the mosque and I sat in a reclining chair on the terrace, listening to the call to prayer and pondering my difficult health situation. All of a sudden, I heard an old man's voice near my right ear: "Get up and hurry to where the call for prayer comes from. There you will find peace and tranquility."

I looked to my right, but nobody was there. Then I heard an old woman's voice near my left ear: "Listen to what the grandfather said. Get up and go."

I looked to my left, but nobody was there. I started feeling nervous and became a bit frightened. Then the old man's voice spoke again: "Go, my son. You are healed."

After these words, I got up and I'm telling the truth when I say that my illness had completely vanished. I ran to the mosque and joined the prayer, and I've never missed a prayer since, *alhamdulillah*. That was 20 years ago.

After embracing Islam, I left work for six months and studied full-time in a traditional Islamic boarding school where I learned all the important basics, including how to read Qur'an. I also got married, and my wife has been one of my most important teachers in Islam.

Reunion

When I visited my family for the first time after being away for 10 years, they were overjoyed. They organized a big gathering and slaughtered a pig as a sign of thanksgiving, as is the custom in East Timor. That's when I had to tell everyone that I had become Muslim and could not join them in eating the pig. They were furious, but I told them that even if they tried to kill me, I would remain steadfast because I had found the truth. They became so enraged that I was forced to run away. I hid in the mosque until after the evening prayer. Then I returned home, went to my room, and locked the door.

In the morning, I told them again that I would not change my religion, regardless of their reaction. My mother calmed everybody down, especially my brothers, who felt they needed to defend our family's honor. She asked if I was happy and I told her yes. Then we hugged, and everyone else followed her peacemaking, *alhamdulillah*.

Science Points to the Existence of God

Professor Jackie Ying is a Singapore-based researcher of nanotechnology who developed the quickest early testing tool for the novel coronavirus (COVID-19) with her team. Professor Ying was born in Taiwan in 1966. As a child, she migrated to Singapore with her parents and went to school there. She is a convert to Islam and says, "If you truly study science, you have to believe in a Creator."

Other Religions Made Her Curious

Professor Jackie Ying received her primary and secondary education in Singapore. She studied in a Chinese stream primary school but attended a more culturally diverse secondary school. It was there that she met people with different belief systems and became curious about religion.

"I always wanted to know the purpose and meaning of life," she said. "And in religion, we find a lot of answers to these questions."

There Must Be a Creator

Professor Ying converted to Islam in her thirties. Asked about the connection between Islam and science, she answers that Islam teaches us to seek knowledge. With scientific knowledge, she said, we can be useful to our societies.

But most importantly, "Scientific knowledge points again and again to the existence of God. So I don't think that the two [religion and science] have a problem with each other."

Being a committed scientist helped Professor Ying to see the truth, the Creator, behind the things she studied.

Professor Ying explains that it was not difficult for her to accept Islam. Unlike other religions, she says, Islam is simple. Other religions have complicated concepts that are difficult to accept, but not Islam. However, despite this simplicity, there is amazing knowledge inside Islam, she adds. "When I first opened the Qur'an, it was clear to me that this was a very, very special and extraordinary book."

Serving Humanity

After performing her first umrah, Professor Ying began covering her head. This showed her belief in Islam and her connection to Allah to everyone. She is also active in *da'wa* work in Singapore. As a scientist, Ying has received dozens of awards and published hundreds of high-ranking academic articles in her field. She currently heads the NanoBio Lab at the Agency for Science, Technology, and Research in Singapore, and was nominated as one of the world's 500 most influential Muslims.

Professor Jackie Ying is a beautiful example of how Muslims contribute to present-day developments, research, and science. Seeing Allah سُبْحَانَهُوَتَعَالَ behind the "scenes" provides her with inspiration to push further, to contribute to, and to serve humanity.

Out of the Mouths of Babies

We learn from our beloved Prophet Muhammad ﷺ that the supplication of a mother is never rejected. And when he was asked whom we should respect, the blessed Prophet ﷺ mentioned the mother three times before mentioning the father. Bella's story reflects these Prophetic teachings in a unique and poignant way.

A few years ago, I found myself distraught over my two sons. One had dropped out of high school and was spending his days sleeping and his nights drinking and looking for trouble in the streets. The other had just been released from a two-year jail sentence. I had no idea how to help them. I had left Columbia fifteen years earlier to seek a better future for my family in the US. I had worked very hard and held multiple jobs, but looking at my two young men, it seemed to have been for naught. Then one day, Jorge came home and I could see in his face that something had happened.

Change

Jorge didn't look at me when he came home that morning, but I remember he seemed different. He was tired and smelled of alcohol and cigarettes, and something felt wrong. He ate some scrambled eggs, had a shower, and went to his room. I followed him, even though I had never bothered him before. I knocked on his door and entered. Jorge sat on his bed, thinking.

I asked him if everything was okay, and he said, "Yeah, Mom." But he had the strangest look on his face. I sat next to him and put my hand on his back. Then Jorge said that he had to give up drinking, that it wasn't good.

I was happy to hear that. After all, that was what I had prayed for all along. I just told him that it was a good idea and left his room. I thought that was it, but actually this confession was only the beginning of a greater change.

A New Friend

From that morning on, Jorge did not drink anymore. He spent most of his time in his room. Sometimes he went out with a friend who picked him up from home. His friend was very polite and always wore a bright white cloth and a small skullcap, and when he smiled, I felt like a light was shining from him.

One day, I invited Jorge's new friend inside for a simple dinner. Jorge and his friend sat down and started talking about God and Jesus and the Virgin Mary. I don't remember everything they said but I was surprised because my son had never talked about God before. I always prayed silently in my room to the Virgin Mary and, through her, to God and Jesus. But I never made it a big issue in our family.

But then the topic turned from Jesus to something else. Jorge revealed to me that he had become a Muslim, and I was shocked.

"Aren't Muslims those terrorists?" I remember asking.

Completely overwhelmed with the situation, I picked up the plates and told them to leave. I admit now that I didn't know what to do. I went to my room and sat down in front of my little shrine. For the first time, I talked directly to God and asked Him for help. Usually, I prayed to the Virgin Mary, but this time was different.

Improvement

I sat there in my room for a long time. I don't remember how many hours, but I was asking God to help me, to help my sons, and to help my family. Jorge did not return for many days, and I began to worry about him. Had I pushed him back to his old lifestyle?

Those days were very difficult for me, but I was also able to reflect. Jorge had changed. He had stopped drinking. He didn't go out at night. He didn't get into fights anymore. Was this all because he had become Muslim? I knew many religious people in my old village who still did bad things like drink heavily and then go to church. But this religion called Islam had changed my son into a good person. I couldn't wait for him to return home. During those days, I prayed more than usual. I asked God to bring Jorge home.

God Returned Us to His Straight Path

After more than two weeks, Jorge returned. His face was shining, and he hugged me, like he had never hugged me before. I was extremely happy and full of joy and hope. Jorge took time to sit down with me. We had long discussions. He told me about the oneness of God and that Jesus was God's Prophet and not His son. I could accept that. He told me about the five daily prayers and other important things in Islam. I took it all in. I could accept Jorge being Muslim now, but when he asked me whether I wanted to accept Islam, I told him that I needed more time.

I thought and prayed for about six more months, and then I accepted Islam at the hands of my son. It was a beautiful moment, *alhamdulillah*. When my other son was released from prison, it

didn't take long for him to also accept Islam, and he has stayed out of trouble ever since. Through Islam, God gave me back my two wonderful sons. He saved them from the violence and destruction of the streets. And He returned us all to His straight path.

Why Didn't Anybody Tell Me?

Seeking closeness to God is not a matter of age. Sincerity is the key, and oftentimes our companions on the path to seeking God can help us develop that sincerity. Greta grew up in a Roman Catholic family of Italian immigrants in the United States and converted to Islam in her seventies at the hands of her beautifully sincere daughter.

I was raised as a Catholic, and my parents were very traditional. We went to church and prayed at home. I was very devout. However, I married a Lutheran man, which upset my parents. I didn't exactly leave the Roman Catholic Church, but I did start joining my husband in his church. I liked the lighthearted ways of the Lutheran church but never really felt at home there either. When my husband became less regular in attending the Sunday service in his church, I started trying out other Christian denominations. My husband didn't mind, and my parents didn't know. The different variations were interesting, but I never found what I was looking for. The truth.

My Most Sincere Prayer

My children grew up. They left the house. My husband passed away. And I was still looking for the right church, the way to the truth. Eventually, I ended up in my local neighborhood church. It was a matter of convenience. I didn't like driving long distances anymore, and the local church was within walking distance. I knew the people, and they also helped me out when I needed help. With all my children living abroad, having help from the young church community made me very happy.

Nevertheless, there was still this desire burning inside my soul, the desire to know the truth. I prayed regularly, and one evening after I came home from church, I just opened my heart to God. I asked Him to guide me. I told Him that I wanted to know the truth. To worship Him as He deserved to be worshipped. It was the most sincere prayer I had ever prayed.

A Surprise Visit

A few weeks later, my daughter visited me from Morocco. We hadn't seen one another for several years, and I was happy but also surprised to see her. She wore a headscarf. When I saw her standing in the door, I was reminded of my prayer to God. And in my heart, I asked myself whether my daughter was bringing the answer to my prayer.

I didn't ask about her headscarf for several days, and she didn't mention anything either. One afternoon, I saw her performing the ritual prayer of the Muslims. She was in prostration, and I quickly closed the door so as not to disturb her. The image of my daughter kneeling with her head on the floor impressed me deeply, and again I wondered if God had sent her as an answer to my prayer.

Why Had No One Told Me About This Earlier?

One evening after dinner, I finally asked my daughter if she was still a Christian. She said no, and we had a very long talk about her journey. She brought the Bible, the Qur'an, and her notebook and explained everything to me. She talked about Jesus ﷺ and our Prophet Muhammad ﷺ. I just listened to her. Tears kept flowing down my cheeks. I was certain that it was God who had sent her to me now as the answer to my prayer. He was guiding me to the truth. When she had finished her detailed explanations, I just hugged her, and asked her why no one had told me about this earlier.

I Became Muslim to Get Married, Then Allah Opened My Heart

We all sometimes catch ourselves judging people by their outward appearance. We know this is wrong because we cannot look into a person's heart, and we don't know what Allah has planned for a person in her future—or for us in our future. This is Cindy's story. It took her five years after becoming Muslim to actually identify as a Muslim publicly. She is a mom of five and lives in Austria.

I had a difficult time as a teenager. I lived with different foster parents and dropped out of school. I was also a teen mom. I wasn't happy and I worried about what my dismal-seeming future would bring. I tried to be a good mom, but I had no support from my family.

One day, I met the man who would become my husband. He was much older than I was, but he cared about me. He was Muslim, and although he did not practice Islam, he told me that in order to get married, I would need to become Muslim. Otherwise, his family would not accept us. For the first time in my life, I felt that somebody truly cared about me, so I accepted Islam to be with my husband. It was the best decision of my life.

Was That the Islam I Had Accepted?

Five years after I formally said my *shahāda* and we got married, I met an old childhood friend who had also become Muslim. But unlike me, she covered her head, prayed, read Qur'an, and fasted. She radiated a special light. She talked about God and His love for us and our love for Him. I was just astonished. *Was that the Islam I had accepted to get married to my husband?* I became truly interested in learning more.

My Way to Allah

The first thing my friend taught me was to say the *shahāda* again. This time with true conviction. Then I slowly learned the prayer. I'm dyslexic and it has not been easy for me to learn the words and verses I have to recite in prayer. But *alhamdulillah*, due to God's infinite mercy, I'm now able to fluently recite al-Fatiha, the opening chapter of the Qur'an. I try to pray all five daily prayers and I recently started wearing the headscarf as well. My progress might be slow, but I believe from the depths of my heart that Allah knows my struggles, and He knows every little, tiny step I take to become a better Muslim.

What I Found in Islam

Practicing Islam has changed my life. I finally feel that I belong. It is a glorious feeling to know that, basically, I have a very big Muslim family. I found the stability and peace I had lacked since childhood.

I want my children to have a good example to follow. I want them to see their mom pray, to see her love for Allah سُبْحَانَهُوَتَعَالَى. I want to show them an example of an upright and honest Muslim woman. I pray every day that they follow me in living and loving Islam.

The Effects of Living Islam

Since I started living Islam, my husband has also started to slowly come back to his faith. Although he never left Islam, he did not practice for many years. *Alhamdulillah*, last year we fasted Ramadan together. It was beautiful, and I felt so many blessings rain down on my family. I pray we will continue to walk together on this path of drawing closer to Allah عَزَّوَجَلَّ.

A French Convert

Sometimes we feel hesitant to practice our religion in the presence of people of other faiths. We retreat to a private room to pray or keep a low profile while we pray silently, at light speed. But it could be our joyous, "out loud" practice of our faith that brings someone closer to Allah. This is the story of how Camille embraced Islam in her home country of France.

I grew up in a traditional French family in a small town in the south of France. My family is Catholic, but except for traditional holidays, religion did not play a big part in our life. Belief is a private matter in France. And although my parents would profess Catholicism, this didn't mean they lived a different lifestyle than my friends' parents who did not believe in God at all. When I was in secondary school, there was this one Muslim girl in my class. Nobody wanted to be friends with her, but I felt sorry for her. My parents had taught me to be kind to everybody, no matter their hair or skin color or where they came from. I struck up a friendship with her. She was very smart and helped me with math, which was my worst subject in school.

Twice a week, we studied together at my house. One day, when I was 15 years old, we couldn't study at my house, so Maryam invited me to study at hers. They lived in a small apartment and Maryam didn't have her own room, so we had to study in the living room. Her mom was very friendly and had prepared some food for us. While we studied, Maryam's mom read from a book in the other corner of the living room. She tried to read quietly, but I heard the beautiful melody. I asked Maryam what her mom was doing, and she told me that she was reading Qur'an, the holy book of the Muslims. I was surprised by this because I had never heard anybody reciting the Bible in such a melodic way. I asked Maryam's mom to sit closer to us and recite so I could hear more clearly. I didn't understand a word, but I really enjoyed her recitation. In a strange way, it touched my heart. From that day forward, I tried to visit Maryam more often, and each time her mom would recite the Qur'an for me. The more I listened, the more I wanted to know about her religion.

One day, she told me about the five daily prayers, and I was really surprised to learn that she prayed to God five times a day. All I knew up until that point was to make supplications the way Christians do. I asked to see her praying and she allowed me to watch. Witnessing her bow down to God in such a beautiful way planted the seed of Islam in my heart. I asked if I could join her, and without telling me I had to become Muslim first, she invited me to do so. Together with Maryam and her mom I prayed in their living room. I was 16 years old.

Although I didn't officially convert to Islam at that time, practicing the Islamic prayer movements became a habit—a habit which I concealed from my family because I was worried they wouldn't accept Islam.

Maryam and her mom never pushed me to become Muslim. After I finished high school, I moved to Paris to study. It was a huge step and a big change. I chose to study history and the Arabic language because I wanted to learn the language that Maryam's mother read in her beautiful recitations from the Qur'an. My interest in Islam grew and I started to read more about the religion. I also continued my habit of performing the prayer movements. The more I learned about Islam, the more I felt a desire grow in my heart to become Muslim. So around 10 years after I first heard Maryam's mom recite the Qur'an, I embraced Islam.

I didn't tell my family for a long time, and when I finally did tell them, they were shocked. My conversion strained our relationship to a great degree, and for several years I worked very hard to keep in contact with them because they didn't want to see me.

Alhamdulillah, with patience, good will, and God's help, I was able to convince them that I had not become a terrorist and that I was still a good member of French society. I started working for the French government and, although I can't wear my scarf while at work, I wear it during my free time. Having been promoted several times, I now have my own office where I can pray easily. I am living proof that God opens doors if we are persistent and have the right intention.

Part Two

Staying the Course

What Does It Mean to Be a Convert?

Converting to Islam means finding peace, tranquility, and love. It means to finally arrive at what you have been looking for. But coming to Islam is the starting line, not the final goal. Conversion opens a new phase of life that brings with it change and challenges, along with new dreams.

A Lifelong Journey

The act of converting is the starting point of a lifelong journey. A journey to our wonderful Creator. A journey of trying to follow in the footsteps of our beloved Prophet ﷺ. It is a journey on the path of the lovers of Allah and, through the journey, we become one of these lovers.

Semantics

Because converting is a process rather than an event, Dr. Tamara Gray, the founder of Rabata, always stresses the importance of using the word convert rather than revert. The word convert carries the connotation of an ongoing process of improvement, while the word revert means simply returning something to a previous state. In fact, if translated into Arabic, the word revert actually means *murtad*, a person who left Islam. When we understand that, the importance of this semantic choice becomes clear.

One Step at a Time

This understanding that conversion is a process is a blessing and a relief. We know that a process takes time. Being engaged in a process means to move continuously toward a goal, taking one step at a time, with patience. No one can understand or implement everything overnight. Implementing each thing we learn in our daily life before moving on to the next step is better for us in the short and long terms than trying to perform an instantaneous "presto chango."

Realism

Trying to implement everything all at once can be overwhelming, and some people wind up taking five steps forward and three steps back. This is unhealthy and discouraging. A sister who recently converted to Islam told me that she sets small goals for herself. For example, she set a goal of covering her head within three months' time. She planned to start praying *tahajjud* over the summer. This way, she said, with each step she took, she had the time to make it a part of her heart and identity before she took the next step.

Living Proud

Showing your Muslim identity requires confidence. Praying requires confidence. Expressing your love for and relationship with Allah سُبْحَانَهُ وَتَعَالَى requires confidence. Maintaining different values than those around you requires a *lot* of confidence. But Allah chose you to be a follower of His most beloved, Prophet Muhammad صَلَّى ٱللَّهُ عَلَيْهِ وَسَلَّمَ, and you can grow into a proud Muslim. To boost your confidence, try reading the *sira* of our beloved

Prophet ﷺ. You will see that he and his companions faced challenges and trials—both personally and as a group—with confidence in Allah and in their new faith.

You can also read about the great achievements of Islamic civilizations. Did you know that the oldest university in the world was founded by a Muslim woman? It's in the *Guinness Book of World Records*. Many innovations in the medical, astronomical, and mathematics fields were made by Muslims. In choosing Islam, you have become a member of a great civilization that you can be proud of.

Share the Peace

Sharing the story of how you came to Islam inspires others and can rekindle your own love for the faith. Share the peace you have found in Islam. Talk to people about how Islam changed your life. Show the best sides of your new and old self.

Not only do conversion stories help those who may be considering Islam, they can also inspire heritage Muslims (those born into Muslim families) to reconnect with Islam and their Creator. You are a fresh breeze. Make *du'a* when you tell your story that Allah ﷻ continues to guide you and that He guides others through you.

How to Find Your Place

Along your faith journey, there will be many new things to learn and many new circumstances to negotiate. As new Muslims, we are introduced to new communities, cultures, and people, and we will have to find our place in these communities. This can involve renegotiating our identity a bit, and it's an exciting process. Sometimes we find ourselves all over again! But don't feel that you need to leave your old identity behind.

What Can You Bring to Islam?

Sit down and reflect on your strengths. What talents, skills, or characteristics can you contribute to Islam and to your new way of life? For example, have you always been a hard worker? Then contribute some of your hard work to the Muslim community.

Has it always been easy for you to get up early? Great! Make it a habit to get up for the special *tahajjud* prayer in the last third of the night. Are you a good speaker or writer? Use your talents to educate others and correct misconceptions about Islam. Are you good at baking? We need you, because #MuslimsLoveCake!!! Organize a food bazaar and donate the profits to a good cause or bake something delicious and donate it to a food pantry. Join a meal train for a sister who just had a baby. Start contributing and you will also make new friends.

Represent

Converting to Islam doesn't mean that you have to give up your own culture. You do not have to start eating only South Asian, African, or Turkish food. Just make sure whatever you eat is halal. You don't have to start wearing all black. Keep your style! Just make sure you cover yourself the way Allah سُبْحَانَهُ وَتَعَالَى wants Muslims to cover. You can still ride a bicycle, jog, hike, paint, sew, or whatever else you like to do. Find other Muslims who like similar activities (it's not as hard as you might think). Grab some coffee together. Start a book club. Meet up to go for a walk. And most importantly, keep your ready smile and positive outlook on life.

Find Other Converts

Converting to Islam is a very unique experience. It can create beautiful bonds of friendship, brotherhood, and sisterhood. Find other new Muslims and set up a regular convert circle where you meet for tea and snacks while talking and sharing knowledge about Islam. Motivate one another. If there are no converts in your community, find some online. Sometimes just knowing that another person is currently going through similar experiences helps a lot. I had a beautiful convert community in Germany, and even though I haven't seen many of them for a long time, we still feel connected because we share a similar story and similar challenges.

Be Part of Your Local Muslim Community

Sometimes the people at your local mosque speak another language. Don't let this discourage you. Go anyway! You can also join a regular study circle in your own language. If there are no other Muslims around, consider traveling to meet them. Go to the closest mosque on the weekends or once a month. Make it a regular habit to connect to other Muslims in the same space. There is blessing in sitting with other pious people, and it will support you in your journey. If you can't spend time with the Muslims around you though, don't despair. Your online Muslim friends form just as much a community as the local mosque. You can Zoom with them, join Masjid Rabata if you're a woman, and create or join chat threads dedicated to supporting Muslims around the world.

Take Time Out to Study Islam

One of the best ways to connect to Islam is to study the faith. There are many more avenues for learning now than there were even 10 years ago. Try to find a platform that has genuine teachers and an organized curriculum. Don't limit yourself to random articles or TikTok.

Often you can find a sister or auntie in your community who would be happy to teach you the basics. She doesn't need to be a famous scholar, just somebody with whom you feel comfortable learning. Once you've absorbed the basics, you can graduate to other teachers who can take you to the next level. This is part of the process. Converting to Islam means you become a lifelong learner.

When searching for a teacher or an Islamic studies program, do your research, but also trust your natural instinct. If you have doubts about certain people or things, make it a habit to listen to that inner voice. Find people you feel comfortable with and whom you feel you can trust in your journey of studying Islam.

You Are Part of a Community

Don't forget that you are part of a Muslim community that is almost two billion strong. A community of people who love Allah and the Prophet Muhammad . Be proactive in finding your place in this community of lovers by accepting the help of others and being of service to those who may need you.

Wisdom and Hope in Dealing with Your Non-Muslim Family

Our decision to become Muslim brings with it a lot of new events, moments, questions, lessons, and beauty. We see the world with different eyes. We have to give ourselves time to slowly adapt to our new life, and we must give our families, loved ones, and friends time to adjust as well. Often, we are the only one in our family to accept Islam, and that means we have to take on the responsibility of explaining to our families the very matters that we ourselves have just begun to understand (and may still be struggling to understand ourselves).

Wisdom and Intention

There will be times when we experience difficulties in dealing with family members who haven't yet accepted our conversion to Islam. They may not like that we cover our head. Or they may want us to celebrate Christmas with them. Or they continue drinking alcohol around us. As Dr. Tamara Gray emphasizes, it is important to approach these matters with wisdom.

I am not giving any legal rulings here, but I do believe that we mustn't approach these situations with harshness and distance. For example, if Christmas is an important time for a family to gather and spend time together, we need to understand that shunning them will drive them away. We can negotiate, for example, that we won't be able to join them at church services, but we'll be there for dinner. By doing this, we are respecting and honoring our parents, keeping family ties, and *insha Allah* bringing them closer to Islam. We can make the intention to help our parents and make them happy. Attending that dinner doesn't mean we are celebrating Christmas.

We are, rather, tending to our family ties. This way, *insha Allah*, we can remain close to our family and keep the doors of *da'wa* open to them.

Allah's Mercy

From one hundred parts of His mercy, Allah ﷻ has only sent one part to this world. This one part is divided among all human beings and animals. The love and care of a mother for her baby is a beautiful reflection of it. Allah says that He has reserved the remaining 99 parts of His all-encompassing mercy for the Day of Judgment.

Hope in Allah's Mercy

An extremely difficult situation for a convert Muslim is when a family member dies without having spoken the profession of faith, the *shahāda*. I experienced such a loss recently, despite the fact that I had tried for many years to explain Islam to my grandfather and bring him closer to the *deen*. In the end, however, it was Allah's will that he died without having said the *shahāda* in front of anybody.

In the sadness of my loss, one of my teachers assured me of Allah's immense mercy. While there is a common misconception that we cannot make *du'a* for a person who dies without professing Islam, she assured me that that is not true. Of course, we can make *du'a* for them. We can ask Allah تَبَارَكَوَتَعَالَى in His infinite mercy to accept whatever little faith the person had in his or her heart, and have confidence in His mercy, which He promised us outstrips His wrath. This provided hope and softened my heart.

Inside the Heart

We can never know what is inside a person's heart. Only Allah جَلَّوَعَلَا knows whether a person secretly believes in Him. Maybe, due to different circumstances, a certain person never openly accepted Islam outwardly, but inwardly she has been a believer all her life. So we leave it to Allah and His infinite mercy to accept her as a believer. And this meaningful *du'a* can console our aching hearts.

In addition to *du'a* it is often recommended that we recite Surah Quraysh (Chapter 106) as often as possible for someone who has experienced a tragic loss or other difficulty. This *surah* is known to ease sadness and help bring acceptance to our grieving hearts.

Letter to Non-Muslim Parents

Sometimes, talking to your non-Muslim family can be difficult. The situation appears deadlocked, or you aren't confident enough just yet to engage in lengthy discussions or answer difficult questions. At times like these, one option is to write letters. That way, you have time to think deeply about what you want to say and how you want to word it. You can write, erase, and rewrite. The following are some examples of how you might start an initial or follow-up letter from your heart to theirs. Remember that these are just loose suggestions. Every family is different, as are the issues they face. A letter to a Christian family is different from a letter to a family of another faith or no faith. The most important thing is that you express your love and respect for them. Write about your appreciation for what they've done for you. Try to write in a way that helps them understand your choice.

Dear Mom and Dad,

I'm writing to you because at the moment, writing is easier than talking. I'm worried that I might say the wrong thing, worried that I might get into an argument with you, worried that I might hurt your feelings...

Dear Mom and Dad,

I love you both so much, and I know that it's because of your love that I am here. Because of your guidance and care, I am the person I am today. You are my home in this world, and I'm so thankful that God made you my parents...

Dear Mom and Dad,

After a long search for my spiritual home, I have found peace and tranquility in Islam. Bowing down to God five times a day, submitting to Him and His will, gives me stability, hope, and strength in this world that has become so unstable and unreliable.

My Dear Parents,

I ask for your forgiveness if I ever hurt you, spoke harsh words to you, ignored you, or made you sad. I didn't understand the importance and blessing of parents. In Islam, I've learned that Paradise is under the feet of our mothers, and that we need to respect our mother and father. Going forward, I will try my best to be the best daughter to you.

Dear Mom and Dad,

I know that having a drink is a family tradition on certain festive occasions. Please accept my sincerest apologies for not being able to join you for a drink anymore. I would still love to be with you, though. Maybe we can celebrate together with sparkling cider instead of alcohol?

Dear Mom and Dad,

I used to think that buying a new phone, a new car, or new shoes would bring me happiness. And it did, momentarily. But this happiness never lasted long enough to fill the yawning emptiness inside my soul. I began to realize that the more I bought, the less satisfied I became. I thought something was wrong with me because I couldn't sustain the happiness that things gave me like everybody else seemed to. It was a vicious cycle. Now, I realize that the hole I was seeking to fill was a yearning for a relationship with God, and that we can't be truly happy without Him in our lives...

Find a Gardener for Your Soul

We look for guidance and wisdom in everything we do. We learn to read and write from a teacher. We even learn to walk with a teacher, our mom or dad. We learn how to play sports with a coach. We go to college or university and are taught by professors. We have supervisors in our workplace. If we want to learn something new, we usually turn toward a person that has knowledge in that field. It should be the same in our religion. Allah has taken us from darkness into light, and once we have accepted Islam, having a spiritual teacher who can guide us along the path and in the purification of our heart is a wonderful option in drawing closer to Allah سُبْحَانَهُۥوَتَعَالَىٰ and learning further about this amazing way of life.

Prayer Is a Gift

Our spiritual guides teach us things that we might not understand otherwise. For example, we know that we have to pray five times a day because this is one of the five pillars of Islam. But did we know that the ritual prayer was actually a gift from Allah to the Prophet Muhammad صَلَّىٱللَّهُعَلَيْهِوَسَلَّمَ and his community? After one of my teachers explained this in a lecture, I viewed my daily prayers in a completely different manner. The way he said it, the words he used, the sound of his voice. All of that went straight to my heart and changed my prayer. This is the blessing of having a teacher who is connected to our beloved Prophet ﷺ through a long chain of spiritual teachers. It's worth it to make an effort to connect to one of these spiritual teachers.¹

Learning to Read: Building My Relationship with Qur'an

Shortly after I became Muslim, I met my first Qur'an teacher. She asked me whether I already knew how to read Qur'an, and when I said no her eyes filled with sparkles. She took my hand and said, "I will teach you." I wanted to object that I wasn't ready yet and needed more time to adjust to all the new things in my life. But my teacher was determined. According to her, it was my personal obligation to learn to read the Qur'an as quickly as possible. Furthermore, I needed preparation so I could later teach it to others. From that day forward, we met twice a week in a beautiful campus mosque in the city of Yogyakarta in Indonesia.

The Most Important Surahs

I would drive to the mosque in the serene early mornings. During the first few classes, we focused on memorizing the three most important short *surahs* in the Qur'an. I would drive home trying to recite and memorize them along the way. It was so new to me. The last time I had to memorize anything was in high school. At the same time, I was also beginning to learn the letters of the Arabic alphabet. My teacher made me write every letter hundreds of times. I thought that was strange, but later I understood the

---

1 A great Islamic resource for women is www.rabata.org. For German language courses, visit www.madrasah.de. Two other great resources for learning are seekersguidance.org and yaqeeninstitute.org.

wisdom behind it. In this way, I really learned each letter. My hand became familiar with the letters. My eyes became accustomed to their shapes. It was like the Arabic letters became a part of me.

Read!

The Islamic science of reciting the Qur'an correctly is called *tajwīd*, and I began to learn it from a small booklet called *"Iqra!"* or "Read!" which is a widely used primer in Indonesia. I found it very beneficial to follow this book in addition to my teacher's explanations, however I wouldn't recommend you take up a *tajwīd* booklet and try to learn by yourself. It is through a teacher that we truly understand how the Arabic letters are pronounced. We need to look at the teacher, to see and hear how she forms the letters, because some Arabic letters correspond to sounds that are similar to our own language, while others require that we practice them over and over again.

Speaking of Patience...

It took me some time before I memorized all the letters and their different forms (they look different when they begin a word, appear in the middle, or end a word). It seemed that I moved at a snail's pace. One of the most challenging things for me was correctly reading short vowels. I would try to read and then stop on one letter, elongating its vowel while thinking about the next letter. This could change the meaning of the word, my teacher explained. Better to stop altogether and start again. I tried to follow. It was frustrating—I just wanted to read the Qur'an! My teacher understood my impatience and gave me additional small *surahs* to memorize while I was on my reading journey so I could use them during prayer.

Listening to the Recitation of Qur'an

Listening to the recitation of the Qur'an helped me a lot in improving my own memorization and recitation. Once I got the basic rules of *tajwīd* down, I made it a habit to listen to Qur'an as much as possible. I chose a *qari* (reciter) whose recitation was the most appealing to me and whose pronunciation I could follow easily, and listened to his recordings often. I even kept Qur'an recitation playing at night when I was asleep!

Continuous Effort

After some time in Indonesia, I had to return to my home country. But I still remember one of the most important pieces of advice my teacher gave me. She said to always continue improving my recitation.

"Learn with different teachers. Correct your pronunciation. Because there are surely better teachers than myself," she would say.

And that's what I did. I continued learning *tajwīd* with different teachers. I tried to improve on my weak letters. I tried to become more fluent. I memorized more of Allah's amazing book. And I'm still doing all that today.

Privilege and Obligation

When I first began learning to read the Qur'an, I never thought that one day I'd be teaching *tajwīd* myself. But almost 10 years after my teacher's prediction, my local circle of convert sisters lost their Qur'an teacher. They needed a replacement ASAP and asked me to fill in until a new teacher could be found. It was then that I truly understood my teacher's wisdom. Why she meticulously taught me all the different *tajwīd* rules and encouraged me to continue learning after acquiring the basics. It became my personal privilege and obligation to teach *tajwīd* to these women. I certainly didn't feel qualified, but Allah ﷻ puts us where we need to be to serve Him best, and I am honored to work with these remarkable women.

Reading Is Only the First Step

Learning to read Qur'an is an enthralling journey that connects us directly to Allah's words. But it's only the first step. Many more steps will follow, like studying the meanings of the Qur'an and integrating more and more of the Qur'an into our daily lives. The thought of all that can seem daunting, but the best advice I've heard is to just jump in wherever you are. If you're brand new to Qur'an, learn the letters like I did. If you used to have a good reading habit but have fallen off the wagon, jump right back on. Try to set a small daily goal and slowly increase it. May Allah make it easy for all of us to read His book, love His book, and find it becoming the cornerstone of our character. *Ameen.*

How to Not Get Burdened with Worship

We live in a world that expects us to always give our best. We have to work and/or study and/or care for others and do it all to the best of our abilities and as perfectly as possible. We expend immense energy in all this worldly work, and when we are done with those worldly tasks, we find ourselves exhausted. Sometimes we feel that adding worship time on top of all that is a burden. Even the bare minimum feels heavy, and we try to finish it as quickly as possible. How can we change that?

Worship as an Energizer

We have to transform our worship into an energizer. Unfortunately, we often judge our worship using the same parameters as our worldly tasks. We look at it as just one more thing that needs to be

done. And when we try to squeeze it "on top of" our worldly tasks, we don't apply the same vigor for reaching excellence to it. Why? Because we don't always see the immediate results of our worship. So it becomes necessary to change our paradigm about worship.

Prayer needs to be done, yes, but what does Allah say about prayer? It is first and foremost for ourselves. Prayer is good for us.

> *And recite [O Muhammad] what is revealed to you of the Book and establish Salah [ritual prayer]. Surely Salah restrains from shamelessness and evil. And indeed, remembrance of Allah is the greatest [thing]. And Allah knows what you do.* (Qur'an 29:45)

> *And establish Salah at both ends of the day, and in the early hours of the night. Surely, good deeds erase bad deeds. That is a reminder for the mindful.* (Qur'an 11:114)

The five daily prayers are there to reconnect us with our true purpose. To be Allah's servants. To worship Him.

> *I did not create jinn and humans except to worship Me.* (Qur'an 51:56)

And that doesn't mean that Allah created us for His benefit. Not at all. It means that He created us to know Him. And we get to know Him through salah. When we think of it like this, our five daily prayers can energize us. They help us gain clarity. They give us peace and contentment in this busy world.

> *...those who believe and whose hearts find comfort in the remembrance of Allah. Surely in the remembrance of Allah do hearts find comfort.* (Qur'an 13:28)

If we understand prayer as our spiritual lifeline, we will rush toward it. We will wait for the next prayer. Standing in front of our Lord, communicating with Him, will be our source of strength.

A Wonderful Transformation

We have become accustomed to continuously thinking. If we aren't thinking, we entertain ourselves. There is no down time, no quiet time. Even during our worship, our thoughts run and run. We go through the movements without gaining the spiritual benefits of a God-focused mind and heart. But when we begin to see our prayer as a refuge—a refuge from our own busyness—our thoughts are easier to tame. As a start, we can try to feel our heart's connection to God during prostration. Try to stay in prostration as long as it takes to feel connected to Allah سُبْحَانَهُ وَتَعَالَى. This will be the start of a wonderful transformation from observing prayer as just an obligation to feeling prayer as a personal need.

Other Forms of Worship

Seeing worship as a form of personal need rather than as a burdensome obligation shouldn't prevent us from engaging in the *dunya*. We have our worldly obligations. Our children, spouses, parents, and others have rights over us. And to fulfill these rights and obligations is important. Plus, it is also a form of worship. The key is having sincerity and the right intention. We can feel our connection to our Lord in every task we do. One method is to make the intention every morning to remember Allah throughout the day. And to renew your intention whenever you feel that you need to strengthen your connection to Him.

Know Your Limits

When it comes to worship, it is also necessary to know our limits. We should never try to do everything all at once. If it is easy for you to fast, then you can keep several *sunna* fasts throughout the month or year. However, if fasting is really difficult for you, maybe you can find another form of worship that brings you closer to Allah. You can give extra charity or wake up at night for *tahajjud* prayer. Maybe you can recite more praises on our beloved Prophet Muhammad ﷺ. Know yourself and choose ways to become more beloved to our merciful Lord. You don't have to begin by overburdening yourself with *sunna* acts of worship that bring difficulty to you.

Be Your Own Comparison

To avoid burdening ourselves with worship, it's necessary that we don't continually compare ourselves with others. We have our own strengths and weaknesses, and other people have other strengths and weaknesses. Try to improve yourself regularly, but be kind to yourself. For example, say your goal is to improve your Qur'an recitation. You can do that gradually. If you currently read one page a day, try to increase it to two pages a day. Then, try to keep reading two pages until it becomes easy for you. Once that happens, then you can increase again. Allah loves those acts that are regular or consistent, even if they are small.

May Allah ﷻ lend us guidance and wisdom on how to become more beloved to Him. May He enable us to feel connected to Him during our worship, and may He grant us sincerity and perseverance in our worship. *Ameen.*

Helping Others

Our beloved Prophet ﷺ said, "The best Muslim is the one who is of most benefit to others." So we strive to become kind, to assist others in any possible way. Of course, there are several ways we can benefit others, depending on our own background and personal situation. I always admired the women in my local mosque who prepared the delicious cakes and cookies to be delighted in after Friday prayer, for *iftar*, or on any other auspicious occasion. I

Find a Gardener for Your Soul

always felt they truly benefited others because of the time, money, energy, knowledge, and certainly love they put into making those goodies. During food bazaars, the profits from their baked goods would go to the mosque. No wonder people loved them (both the cookies and their makers).

Unfortunately, I'm not able to make delicious desserts, so I have to devise other means of benefiting others, but I think you understand my point. If you are a student, try to help your classmates. If you are eating in a restaurant, try to keep your place as clean as possible so the person cleaning up doesn't have more work to do than necessary. Help your elderly neighbor to carry their shopping bags or take out the garbage for them. Give your seat to the pregnant lady on the bus. Cook for your sick friend or neighbor. Organize a meal train for a lady who just gave birth to a new baby. Try to think of new, creative ways to be one of the best Muslims by benefiting other people.

Express Lanes on the Spiritual Path

Just like there can be speed bumps on the spiritual path, such as neglecting salah or giving in to temptations, there are also express lanes that can help us get closer to Allah. Allah سُبْحَانَهُوَتَعَالَ created humans with different talents and struggles, so He certainly didn't create Paradise and equip it with only one way of entering it. On the contrary, Allah made Paradise with several doors through which we may enter, depending on which sorts of worship and connection with Him call to us. The following are a few forms of worship that can help us expedite our progress toward a fulfilling spiritual life.

Always Remember Allah عَزَّوَجَلَّ

In Surah Ali 'Imran, Allah encourages us to remember Him in all our circumstances:

> ...those who remember Allah standing and sitting, and [lying] on their sides, and ponder on the creation of the heavens and the earth [saying:] "Our Lord, You have not created all this in vain. We proclaim Your purity. So save us from the punishment of the Fire." (Qur'an 3:191)

When we remember Allah ﷻ and remain aware of the fact that He is All-Seeing, All-Knowing, and All-Hearing, it becomes much more difficult to commit sins, to be unfriendly to people, or to behave unjustly. If we always remember Him in our hearts, on our lips, and in our minds, it becomes easier to be kind and care for those around us. If we are aware of Him, we can discern right from wrong. Our hearts will be able to differentiate.

And if we do something wrong, we will feel sincere remorse for having displeased Allah ﷻ, and we'll quickly turn to Him in repentance, *insha Allah*.

Be Part of the Body

Caring for our Muslim brothers or sisters means that we see them as part of our Muslim family. We care when they have a problem, and we help in any way we can. We make du'a for them, we offer a helping hand, we help them out financially... One beautiful way to help our Muslim brother or sister is by conducting two special prayer cycles for them called salat-ul-hajah. *This special prayer is conducted when one wishes to ask Allah ﷾ for help with a specific need. It can be offered for others as well as ourselves, and our dear Prophet ﷺ told us that "No Muslim servant supplicates for his brother behind his back but that the angel says: 'And for you the same.'" (Saḥīḥ Muslim 2732)*

Share the Pain

Our beloved Prophet Muhammad ﷺ also said that the believers are like one body. When one of the limbs suffers, the whole body responds to it with wakefulness and fever. One right of our Muslim brother or sister is that we visit them when they are ill. Nowadays, we often feel afraid to visit our sick friends and family members. We're afraid the illness might spread, and our society views illness as a sign of weakness. Or we may simply feel we're too busy. But all these excuses come from worldly, even selfish thinking.

A true believer cares enough to visit, no matter the circumstances. Indeed, Allah سُبْحَانَهُوَتَعَالَىٰ will ask some people on the Day of Judgment why they did not visit Him. They will all be surprised and will ask: "Ya Allah, how was I supposed to visit You?" Allah will then answer that they should have visited their sick Muslim brother or sister and that they would have found Allah there.

Sometimes, however, we are unable to visit our sick or struggling brothers and sisters because they are in quarantine or are far away. At times like these we may catch ourselves saying things like, "All I can do is make *du'a*," as if *du'a* is some pathetic last resort. But *du'a* is actually the first and best weapon of the believer. Making *du'a* means going straight to the One who has the power. The One who hears all and knows all and who says "Be," and it is. He will reward us for our intentions to help and for making *du'a*, as He loves to hear our voices raised in trust to Him.

Give Sadaqah

A very important way to help others is to spend on their care. If we are from among those to whom Allah سُبْحَانَهُوَتَعَالَىٰ has not given much wealth, *alhamdulillah*, we should try and spend whatever is possible for us. Of course, if we belong to those people whom Allah عَزَّوَجَلَّ has blessed with abundant wealth, *alhamdulillah*, we should try to spend even more. Feed a hungry person. Clothe a poor person. Spend on an orphan. Help a needy neighbor. But the Prophet صَلَّىٰاللَّهُعَلَيْهِوَسَلَّمَ instructed us to spend first and foremost on our own family members in need. Maybe our elderly parents can't work any longer and need some extra support. Maybe our brother is currently unemployed and has difficulty making ends meet. We should try to help as much as possible. The poor have a right to some of our wealth. And helping other people financially purifies our wealth and helps us become better, kinder people *insha Allah*. And don't forget the most important part—our intention.

We give seeking Allah's pleasure and not asking for the praise or thanks of people.

Give in Good Times

Many people suddenly start giving abundantly once they are ill or close to death. However, our Prophet ﷺ taught us that it is much more meaningful to give when in the midst of life and health. He said that one dirham (silver coin) of charity given when one is healthy counts as more and is better in the sight of Allah, than one hundred dirhams given in charity for a dead person.

Give in Hard Times

A man once came to the Prophet ﷺ and asked him for charity. The Prophet ﷺ did not have anything to give to him, but the man kept insisting on being given charity. The Prophet ﷺ told the man to go to a shop and buy whatever he needed and tell the shop owner to assign the debt to the Prophet ﷺ. Now, when our beloved Prophet said he had nothing to give, he didn't mean that he had nothing *extra*. He meant he had nothing at all. But he ﷺ did not think about his own debt, nor about filling his own stomach; rather his main concern was helping this man who had come asking for charity. So don't wait for better times to come nor for death to approach. If we are alive and healthy, it is the best time to give in charity.

How Should We Give

The Prophet ﷺ taught us that whenever somebody asks charity of us, we should give—even if only a little. Moreover, it is extremely important that we give our charity in the best of manners. Because in reality, Allah ﷻ sent that person to us as an opportunity for us to purify our wealth and gain His pleasure.

So giving in the most beautiful way, without shaming or looking down on the receiver, is part of the worship of charity.

However, it's not only the person who asks charity from us who has a right over some of our wealth, but also the person who does not ask:

> *And in their wealth, there was a right for the one who asks and the one who is deprived.* (Qur'an 51:19)

> *And those in whose riches there is a specified right for the one who asks and the one who is deprived.* (Qur'an 70:24-25)

The latter we must search for ourselves. If you hear someone lost their job, you can send an anonymous gift card their way, for example. These secret acts of charity will beautify both our hearts and our graves.

Giving to Those Close to You

When giving charity, many of us forget the people close to us. However, our needy family members, neighbors, friends, or colleagues should actually be given priority. Our Prophet Muhammad ﷺ said that when we give to the poor, we give charity only, but when we give to our family members, we give charity *and* keep family ties. For example, if our uncle needs help to pay for his children's food or schooling, we should give to him before donating to others, because he belongs to our family. Likewise, if our parents need financial assistance, we should endeavor to relieve their burden before sending money to an organization.

Giving in Charity Spreads Happiness and Keeps Calamities Away

Many times, our beloved Prophet Muhammad ﷺ mentioned the virtue of giving charity in connection with forgiveness and protection from calamities in both this life and the next. Giving charity can wipe away our sins and protect us from dying at a time when we are distant from Allah سُبْحَانَهُ وَتَعَالَى.

Perhaps because a person regularly gives in charity, Allah عَزَّوَجَلَّ may keep thieves away from their house or keep them in good health. It is possible that in response to someone's habit of feeding others, Allah جَلَّ وَعَلَا will keep discord away from her family. Giving to people who have less than we do will never diminish our wealth and provision. On the contrary, it will only bring blessings and goodness into our lives and the lives of our families.

Giving in charity because we want to help other people, because we want to relieve a small part of their heavy burden, or because we want to give them some happiness in difficult times is immensely rewarding. Giving makes us feel good. So whenever we feel a bit down or even depressed, we should try to make someone else happy. This will surely cheer us up, *insha Allah*.

The Real Spirit of Spiritual Growth

There was a time when I thought that in the blessed month of Ramadan, everything should be perfect, or at least close to perfection. There should be no disturbances, no difficulties, no noise because I wanted to focus on Ramadan. I thought that Ramadan should be a quiet time where it was only me and the Qur'an. Me and tarawīh prayer. Me and fasting. And many times, I was disappointed when it did not turn out the way I had imagined it should be.

Reality Check

One year we lived in a small, quiet village in Indonesia. A perfect place for a perfect Ramadan. But just as the holy month started, a clangorous construction site began right next to us. There went my perfect Ramadan. Other years, I looked forward to joining *tarawīh* prayers, but my tranquility there was shattered by children crying, shouting, and setting off firecrackers. Later, I had to miss *tarawīh* altogether to care for my baby daughter, who was very particular about her sleep at night. And it went on and on. I'm usually quick to understand a message, however my idea of Ramadan as a time of quiet spirituality had yet to be revised and adjusted. It wasn't until my eleventh Ramadan, which began with a toothache and a sleepless first night, that I learned the lesson Allah سُبْحَانَهُ وَتَعَالَى had been teaching me all along.

Embrace the Challenges

I finally understood that Ramadan is not a retreat. Ramadan *is* about spiritual growth, but *spiritual growth happens in many different ways.* At the beginning of one Ramadan, my three-year-old daughter came down with a fever and could not eat or sleep at night for five days. I tried to embrace that challenge. After her recovery, she and her older brother fought like cats and dogs. My son can be super moody, and every minor thing that wasn't in line with his view of the world at the moment upset him. It was irritating. It was annoying. But I tried to embrace it. I guess that is where I needed spiritual growth—in embracing life's (and Ramadan's) challenges. Truly, Allah عَزَّوَجَلَّ knows best!

A Time to Grow

As I began to understand that Allah عَزَّوَجَلَّ sent me all these situations to mold into me a better and more mature person, I found the quietness and solitude of Ramadan that I had been looking for—inside of me. And I learned that is what Ramadan is all about. It is not just about reading Qur'an, but struggling to find the time to read Qur'an while working full-time, organizing the house, taking care of the kids, and trying to prepare to move. It is not just about attending *tarawīh* prayer in a relaxed and quiet atmosphere, but about praying *tarawīh* no matter what the circumstances inside or outside. I realized that there is no perfect time for remembering Allah جَلَّ جَلَالُهُ. We just have to remember Him all the time, wherever we are, whatever we are doing or experiencing. I understood that just because it is Ramadan, the world does not stop moving so that I can have my perfect spiritual month. I have to make each Ramadan my perfect Ramadan.

We Are Women of God

All of us know the uncomfortable stares. The looks of pity. People who click their tongues when they see a Muslim woman. The whispers. Even the snide remarks. And all of this because we cover our heads. Because we wear a piece of fabric around our heads and chests. We dress modestly because we follow our Lord. We follow His commands because we are sure, we are most certain, that whatever Allah سُبْحَانَهُوَتَعَالَ has decreed for us is best. However, sometimes facing negativity daily requires some reassurance. We need some backup. We need support to boost our self-confidence.

To Be Recognized

Allah عَزَّوَجَلَّ tells us in the Qur'an that we should cover ourselves so that we become known:

> O Prophet, tell your wives and your daughters and the women of the believers to bring down over themselves [part] of their outer garments. That is more suitable that they will be known and not be abused. And ever is Allah Forgiving and Merciful. (Qur'an 33:59)

Allah wants us to be recognized as believing women. A few years ago, I traveled from Germany to Poland by train. I wore an ivory headscarf and a long dress. All of a sudden, the train stopped in the middle of nowhere. It was quite a while before we got moving again. While the train was at a standstill, people began chatting with one another. At one point, a man asked me which Christian order I belonged to. I was quite surprised by his question. I told him that I was Muslim and that's why I covered myself. It was his turn to be surprised! Another time, I was asked a similar question upon arrival at the airport in my hometown. These two incidents made me ponder. People thought I was a Christian nun, and that made me proud, because I was happy that people recognized me as a woman close to God. But at the same time, I was sad because people didn't think that a white, European woman could be Muslim—or that a Muslim woman would cover for the same beautiful reason as a nun.

A friend of mine related a similar story. When she returned home to her village to visit her family, an old man came running toward her, crying. He was so touched by her appearance. She wore a long dress and a light-colored head scarf. Later, her mother told her that the old man had thought she looked just like the Virgin Mary—Maryam, the mother of Prophet Isa عَلَيْهِمَاٱلسَّلَام (peace be upon them). Similar to Maryam عَلَيْهَاٱلسَّلَام (peace be upon her), Muslim women show their love and obedience to Allah جَلَّجَلَالُهُ through their dress. Of course, there are many ways to do that, but dressing in a manner pleasing to Allah عَزَّوَجَلَّ is certainly one special form of showing our love and obedience to Him.

Beautiful Reason

These encounters illustrate one reason that Allah جَلَّوَعَزَّ ordained that Muslim women cover. Allah wants us to be known as women of God. He wants us to be a reminder to the people. He wants people who see us to remember Him. Of course, there are many other reasons for and wisdoms behind Allah's decision for women to cover. However, we should especially remember this point. Why? Because when we are the target of people's stares or comments, we can remember that they are not the ones we are aiming to please. We want to be recognized as Muslim women because of Him. We want every single person who sees us to be reminded of our amazing Creator. *That's* why we do it.

Allah, Islam, and Our Priorities

To have priorities in life is important and natural. All of us have them, but do we take time to reflect on them? What is our main priority? Why is it number one? For many of us, our main priority is usually work or studies. For many others, it may be family, children, or friends. Ideally, we arrange our life according to our priorities, which can change as we grow.

The Choice Between Class and Allah

When I studied in Germany after my conversion to Islam, Allah عزّوجلّ taught me what He wants my priorities to be. The prayer times in Germany pose different challenges throughout the year, as is the case in many other places in the Northern Hemisphere. In summer, the days are extremely long and the nights are very short. In winter, the days are short and the dark hours of the night are very long. It was my first winter in Germany after accepting Islam that I realized the tremendous importance of prayer in my life.

The midday prayer, Dhuhr, started at 12:30 p.m., and the afternoon prayer, Asr, started at 1:35 p.m. There was just one hour to get my midday prayer done. However, I had class from 12 to 2 pm. *Alhamdulillah*, I was resolute in making Allah the most important priority in my life. There was no excuse. I had to go and meet Him despite the fascinating heated discussions in class. I stepped out of the classroom and onto my portable prayer room—my prayer carpet. I talked to my Lord, bowed down to Him, and showed Him that He is my first priority in life.

Kids

The second example that illustrates the importance of getting our priorities straight comes from one of my best friends. When she had her first baby, she told me she often struggled with observing the prayer times. Whenever she put the baby down to try and pray, he would scream at the top of his lungs. So she would delay her prayer. However, once when the time for one particular prayer was almost up, she decided to put her baby down to pray—even though he was screaming. Thirty seconds into her prayer, he was asleep. *Subhan Allah*! This drove home for her that her prayer—her connection with her Creator—was the most important thing in her life, and that nothing should come between Him and her.

Created to Worship

There are many other examples that can be cited to illustrate this point. Being a Muslim means to fully submit to Allah سُبْحَانَهُ وَتَعَالَى. It means to set our priorities straight. It means that Allah, His Prophet صَلَّى ٱللَّهُ عَلَيْهِ وَسَلَّمَ, and His religion should naturally be our first priority. Why? Because we love Allah. We love His Messenger and we love the religion He gifted us. It is because of Allah that we feel peace and tranquility in our hearts. It is because of Him that we are able to breathe, eat, move, and live.

Observing our five daily prayers should never be a burden upon us. Rather, we should run toward it. It is a relief from our worldly life. It helps us to reset our priorities. It constantly reminds us of what is truly important in this life. Allah created us for the purpose of worshipping Him. That's it. That's our task. That's our purpose. Everything else comes after that. "Allah is greater" than every other responsibility, every other work, task, joy, or hobby. Those all come after we have fulfilled our main purpose in life. Realizing this can bring true submission and tranquility to our life. This doesn't mean that we forsake all of our other responsibilities, but it reminds us that everything else is temporary.

Allah Is in Control

Allah reminds us in the Qur'an that our property and our children are a test for us:

> *And know that your wealth and your children are only a test and that with Allah is a great reward.* (Qur'an 8:28)

He warns us against letting our wealth and children divert us from the remembrance of Him:

> *O believers! Do not let your wealth or your children divert you from the remembrance of Allah. For whoever does so, it is they who are the losers.* (Qur'an 63:9)

When we remember to make our most merciful Creator our first priority, we hand ourselves, our problems, and responsibilities over to Him. When we put Allah سُبْحَانَهُ وَتَعَالَى and His religion first, everything else will fall into place. No matter what comes our way, we have our prayer, we have Allah to fall back on. We don't have to manage, control, and understand everything. That's not our main purpose in this life. Allah is able to manage everything. He is in control and He understands everything. We just have to worship Him. May He guide all of us to perfect our prayers. *Ameen.*

A Mercy for the World

When I embraced Islam in early 2008, saying the two shahādas was part of the process. I bear witness that there is no god but God, and I bear witness that Muhammad is His messenger. To this day, I'm still in the process of trying to understand the extent and greatness of these two statements. Honestly, learning about our beloved Prophet Muhammad ﷺ was not the first thing on my agenda after I embraced Islam. This is something I'd do differently today. In retrospect, learning about our beloved Prophet Muhammad ﷺ and building a personal connection with him from the very beginning would have made some things easier. Why do I say that?

The Prophet Said

As new Muslims, we are sometimes overwhelmed by all the novel teachings and practices and confused by the diversity in what we thought would be straightforward. We read about Islam in an unstructured way from the internet, hear about rules and mores from people at the mosque, and try to understand books that are given to us. It can feel piecemeal and turns out to put the cart before the horse. Today, I wish that somebody would have told me to nurture my connection to our Prophet Muhammad ﷺ

as, or even before, I worked on the other aspects of Islam. I wish that somebody would have taken me by the hand and told me about the amazing person our Prophet ﷺ was, all the heartwarming and heartbreaking stories from his life. Instead, I only had access to narrations from our beloved Prophet ﷺ and what he said. Although I tried to follow his words, I wasn't able to fully connect. I felt distant from him and unable to connect him to my present moment.

How to Build a Connection

This missing connection hurt me, but I didn't really know how to change it. I wondered how I could better follow and imitate him. Then, Allah سُبْحَانَهُۥوَتَعَالَىٰ sent me my first spiritual guide. He was able to help me connect with our Beloved ﷺ because he himself had already forged a connection with him. My teacher began by filling in some of the experiences behind the words of the Prophet ﷺ, and this brought him to life for me. Seeing the deep, sincere emotion in my teacher's face as he spoke of his beloved Prophet brought a missing dimension to my life as a Muslim.

Learning About Our Prophet

After hearing my teacher's explanations, I knew that I wanted this connection. I wanted those feelings. But it was still difficult for me to feel a personal connection with our beloved Prophet ﷺ. Then, I started reading the *sīra*—books about the life of the Prophet. Now, there are quite a few books written about his life. One of my teachers recommended reading Martin Ling's *Muhammad: His Life Based on the Earliest Sources*. It is written in an accessible way and its aim is to connect the reader's heart with our beloved Prophet ﷺ. I was especially impressed by the way our Prophet Muhammad ﷺ treated people who did not treat him well. He showed mercy to those who did not show mercy to him. My respect and adoration for the Prophet began to blossom.

Stories of Strength and Mercy

It was the Prophet's ﷺ character, strength, and mercy found in the stories of the *sīra* literature that really touched my heart. I began feeling a bond develop between my heart and our beloved Prophet Muhammad ﷺ. For example, a story that touched me deeply was about a blind Jewish beggar whom the Prophet ﷺ fed regularly, even though he spoke badly about him. The beggar wasn't aware that the man he was maligning was the one feeding him. But the Prophet ﷺ continued to do so, and in such a soft, gentle, and merciful way—like no other human being. Our beloved Prophet ﷺ fed him every morning with his own hand, even though this beggar would always curse him and speak ill of him. And he never revealed who he was.

After our Prophet Muhammad ﷺ passed away from this temporary world, his closest companion Abu Bakr al-Siddiq ﷜ went to feed this beggar. He had heard from his daughter, the Prophet's wife, that that was one of the deeds of the Prophet ﷺ and he wished to carry on with it. Once Abu Bakr al-Siddiq ﷜ started feeding him, the beggar immediately recognized that it was not the same person giving him food. The beggar then described how he always held the hand of the person feeding him, and described how he would make the food fine before feeding it to him. Abu Bakr ﷜ cried and informed the blind beggar that the Prophet ﷺ was no more. How can we not love our Prophet ﷺ when this was his character? And how can we understand our faith well if we don't know him?

My Muslim Name

When I became Muslim in 2008, I met a Muslim man whom I interviewed for my work. While talking, I disclosed to him that I had become Muslim a few weeks earlier, and the first thing he asked was: "What is your Muslim name?" His question puzzled me. I didn't know that I needed a Muslim name. But then, I also didn't know much about Islam at that time. I didn't cover, didn't know how to pray, and didn't know about the whole halal meat thing either.

A Muslim Name

The man seemed very excited and insisted: "Well...you need a Muslim name." I told him that I didn't know any Muslim names for women. He was incredulous. We sat in a small Muslim-owned business—a restaurant/travel agency—in Cambodia. I looked around the place and saw the name plate of the travel agent on her desk. It read "Azizah."

"I like that name," I told him. "Azizah. That's a good name," he agreed. And that's how I got my Muslim name. It was like many other incidents in my life, not really a matter of choice, but rather a matter of Allah's *qadr*. I didn't even know the meaning of Azizah, but when I met new people, especially Muslims, and they asked my name, I answered with confidence "Azizah," and everybody seemed pleased.

Why Do You Need an Additional Name?

Of course my family, who are non-Muslim, weren't quite as pleased. My mom, especially, was upset about me having an additional name. She didn't understand why I had to change the name that she had so carefully chosen for me. I told her that in the family I would still be Claudia, but that didn't make her feel any better. She didn't like my writing being published under my Muslim name and she didn't like it when my Muslim friends called me Azizah. My husband, to respect and honor my parents, chose to use my German name. He still does now.

Two Names for Two Selves?

In a strange way, I felt that having a Muslim name created something close to having two identities. I was Azizah with my Muslim friends and Claudia with my non-Muslim family. Did Claudia also pray? Or was it Azizah who prayed? Was Claudia even Muslim? Was Claudia expected to be different from Azizah? My awareness of the dilemma of using different names in different circumstances grew slowly. When I met new Muslim people, I would make this introduction: "My Muslim name is Azizah but my German name is Claudia." So, was Azizah not German? I didn't know if anybody else had shared an experience similar to mine with their names, but it became difficult for me to reconcile the two names.

Becoming Whole

I wasn't less Muslim when I used my German name, nor was I more Muslim when I used Azizah. So I began to realize that I didn't need a Muslim name to declare my Muslim identity. But because many of my Muslim friends already knew me by Azizah, I couldn't really drop the name altogether. And in a way, the name Azizah defined a part of me, just like Claudia did, and just like other names ascribed to me like "mama" or "doctor" or "teacher" did. For me, realizing that Claudia is fully and wholly Muslim was an important step. I can be Muslim with a German name. There is no problem with that. Having a Muslim name is part of my conversion process. At one point during that process, having a Muslim name was very important to me. Today, I like to use both names. Especially in Muslim circles I like to use Claudia Azizah.

Re-embracing My German Name

Re-embracing my German name was an important step in merging my German and Muslim identities into one. I'm a native German, born to German parents, and I grew up in Germany. My German name is part of that personal history, which eventually led me to Islam. It was Claudia who accepted Allah's call to follow His beautiful religion. Why should I drop this name altogether? Being away from home and advancing in age helped me discover that certain features of my culture are very dear to me, and that being a German Muslim is who I am.

Don't Follow Other People

Everybody needs to find his or her own way in approaching the issue of names. We can always change our preferences, and we don't have to follow other people's preferences. We can keep the name our parents gave us as long as it is a nice name with a good meaning. We can adopt a Muslim name. Or we can have two names. It is just important to keep in mind that our decision has an effect on our surroundings and especially on our family. Recently my mother told me that she saved my Indonesian phone number under Claudia Azizah. *Subhan Allah.*

Getting the Right Balance

If our life is in balance, we feel content and happy. If our life is out of balance, we feel distressed, nervous, unhappy, and unfulfilled. Finding the right balance is essential to living our life with purpose and growing with the light of faith Allah has gifted us.

Priorities

To achieve balance means that we understand our priorities and progress toward them continually. Our main priority as Muslims is Allah—worshipping Him and following His teachings as best we can. Balance means that we have a goal in mind. We get up when we fall. We try to keep our balance and move forward, even though we may stumble.

Balance Between This World and the Next

What does it mean to follow the straight path and find balance in it? It means that we try to find a balance between our life in this world and the life that awaits us in the next world. We realize that this world is transitional. Our beloved Prophet Muhammad ﷺ advised us to: "Be in this world as though you were a stranger or a traveler." In his narration of this hadith, Ibn Umar added: "When evening comes, do not expect (to live till) morning, and when morning comes, do not expect (to live till) evening. Take from your health (a preparation) for your illness, and from your life for your death" (Ṣaḥīḥ Bukhari 6416).

A wayfarer is always busy planning and preparing for the journey ahead, so what are the preparations we should make for our journey from this life to the next?

The five daily prayers are an absolutely essential provision for the next world and the key means to balancing our life between this world and the next.

Giving charity is another important part in preparing for the next phase of our journey. It helps us erase the love of this world from our hearts and helps us focus on what pleases Allah ﷾ and helps other people.

Seeking sacred knowledge is another effective way to balance our life and prepare for our journey. It helps us reduce heedlessness, as time we used to spend shopping or binge-watching our screens becomes dedicated to increasing our knowledge of Islam, and thus our love for it. Seeking knowledge blesses our time, increases our energy, and redirects our focus away from this world.

Endeavor to be in the company of devoted believers and scholars. Sitting with them, for lessons or even other kinds of gatherings, brings our hearts nearer to our Lord and makes it easier to focus on doing good.

How to Regain Balance

Sometimes, due to different circumstances, we lose balance in our life. How can we right ourselves when this happens?

As quickly as possible, we need to reconnect to Allah ﷾ on a daily basis. Check your five daily prayers:

Are you praying all of them?

Are you praying them on time?

Try to pray them as early as possible. Don't delay. Don't wait for the movie to finish first and then pray.

Keep your *wudu* as much as possible. This both keeps you in a protected and purified state and makes it easier to pray as soon as the *adhan* sounds.

Allocate some extra time that is only for Allah and yourself. Nobody else should have part in this time. Perform some extra *sunna* prayers. You can do the pre-noon prayer, Salat al-Duha, or the night vigil, *tahajjud*. Do some extra *tahlil* (reciting *la ilaha illa Allah*) or *salawat* (reciting praises on our beloved Prophet Muhammad ﷺ). And try to recite abundant *istighfar*, seeking Allah's forgiveness. You don't have to do all of these, but choose one or two acts of worship and remembrance that speak to your heart.

How Knowledge Can Make Us More Spiritual

The very first word of revelation to our beloved Prophet Muhammad ﷺ was the word "Iqra!" This is an imperative command and means "Read!" This very first word of revelation points to an extremely important part of our religion, which is knowledge. We read to obtain knowledge. But why is knowledge so important in Islam? Because it is only through knowledge that we can do what Allah سبحانه وتعالى expects of us. It is only through knowledge that we know our place on this earth and our role as human beings. It is only through knowledge that we can worship Allah as He wants us to worship Him. And it is only with knowledge that we can become true spiritual beings. It is through knowledge, acting on that knowledge, and the correct intention, sincerity, and perseverance in our actions that knowledge can transform us into spiritual beings and make us better Muslims and more beloved to Allah عزوجل.

Acting Upon Our Knowledge

There exists a difference between knowledge and information. We live in a world that is flooded with all kinds of information, including information about Islam. Anybody can open the Internet and find the *information* he or she is looking for. However, the difference between knowledge and information is that knowledge becomes a part of a person. Only by acting upon what we have learned does information become knowledge. And once we act upon our knowledge, Allah سُبْحَانَهُوَتَعَالَى will grant us more knowledge. Our Prophet Muhammad صَلَّىٱللَّهُعَلَيْهِوَسَلَّم said that if Allah wishes good for a person, He grants him understanding in religion (Islam). We should always make supplication to Allah to gift us with sacred knowledge:

> So high [above all] is Allah, the Sovereign, the Truth. And, [O Muhammad], do not hasten with [recitation of] the Qur'an before its revelation is completed to you, and say, "My Lord, increase me in knowledge." (Qur'an 20:114)

No Spirituality Without Sacred Knowledge

If we aim to become true servants of Allah سُبْحَانَهُوَتَعَالَى, we have to endow ourselves with sacred knowledge. We have to learn how we can please Allah. How to clean and polish our souls. If we long for more spirituality in our lives, we have to seek sacred knowledge. We need to learn more about this beautiful religion. We need to know what is pleasing to Allah and what is abhorrent in the eyes of Allah. We need to start with the basics and slowly work our way up. We can't expect to feel true love and longing for Allah عَزَّوَجَلَّ if we still engage in major sins. It's best to have a genuine spiritual teacher who can guide us on this path to remake ourselves for Allah.

Never Stop Seeking Knowledge

Once we have managed the basics, have become firm in our obligatory acts, and have abstained from the major sins, we should start searching for more knowledge on how we can make ourselves more pleasing to Allah سُبْحَانَهُوَتَعَالَى. We need to learn how to become a better servant of Allah. This is an ongoing process. Our beloved Prophet Muhammad صَلَّى ٱللَّهُ عَلَيْهِ وَسَلَّمَ said that we should aim to seek knowledge from the cradle to the grave. Because by continuously seeking knowledge we acknowledge that we still haven't reached the goal. We still haven't arrived where Allah wants us to be. That is the beauty of Islam. You can always attain more: more knowledge, more piety, more spirituality, more love, more obedience. The seeker of sacred knowledge will always feel thirsty for more knowledge.

To Seek Knowledge Is Our Human Nature

Allah has created humanity with one of His most important characteristics, which is knowledge. Allah is the Most Knowledgeable. He is All-Knowing. When Allah created the first human being and prophet, Adam, He taught him all the names and gave him knowledge. The scholars of Islam explain that this includes worldly knowledge, as well as knowledge about Allah عَزَّوَجَلَّ, and the names of Allah. This demonstrates that we have been created to learn and to obtain knowledge. This sacred knowledge about Allah has been reserved for human beings. It is a light that Allah bestows on those who seek it.

Knowledge Is Light

Our Prophet Muhammad صَلَّى ٱللَّهُ عَلَيْهِ وَسَلَّمَ said that knowledge is light and what he meant was that sacred knowledge, knowledge about our religion, will bring light into our lives. Sacred knowledge illuminates our hearts. If we make an attempt to seek sacred

knowledge and depart on the path of knowledge, we will see that darkness leaves our life. We will feel closer to Allah. Our prayers will become more focused. We will be able to better understand what Allah is telling us in His beautiful book. We will begin to see in His creation more signs of His wonderful power and tremendous might. We will find it more difficult to do things that are not pleasing to Allah. And once this shining light of knowledge enters our hearts and lives, it will *insha Allah* also illuminate our surroundings, our families, and our communities. We will be able to spread this light of knowledge to the people around us.

All knowledge comes from Allah, and we should always be grateful for any beneficial knowledge that we obtain. One way to express our gratitude is to perform two prayer cycles to show our beloved Lord how grateful we are for what He has given to us. And when we are grateful for the knowledge we are given, *insha Allah*, He will give us more. More knowledge and more light to make us shine like a bright star.

How to Find Sweetness in Prayer

Prayer is an essential and central part of our everyday life as Muslims. We pray five times a day, thirty-five times a week, and around 1,825 times a year. How can we make the most of this precious gift Allah ﷻ has given us? How can we truly feel connected to Allah, the most Merciful? How can we go beyond the mere movements, and be present with our hearts, and feel the pleasure that comes with this connection? How can our hearts feel the rest, peace, and tranquility in His remembrance? It is through the sweetness of prayer.

> *Those who believe and whose hearts find comfort in the remembrance of Allah. Surely in the remembrance of Allah do hearts find comfort.* (Qur'an 13:28)

What Does Sweetness of Prayer Mean?

One way to understand "sweetness of prayer" is through the Arabic word, *khushu*. It is mentioned in the Qur'an as a sign of a successful believer to have *khushu* in his/her prayer.

> *Successful indeed are the believers: those who humble themselves in prayer...* (Qur'an 23:1-2)

Khushu means to have full concentration in prayer, focusing only on Allah, being humble and submissive in prayer. It's this feeling that perfects our prayer and connects us to our Creator. It means that we will try to forget everything about this world and focus only on Allah. If we succeed in performing such a prayer, we will feel refreshed. Our spiritual batteries will be recharged. We'll be filled with spiritual light that illuminates our actions, words, and thoughts. And *insha Allah*, we will belong to the successful ones.

How Can We Achieve This Sweetness?

To achieve the sweetness of prayer is not impossible. However, it might require some time. It might happen only once in a while, and it might need some work. For some people, it might just come naturally. However, all of us should make a serious effort to feel *khushu*, sincerity and sweetness, in prayer. Here are a few practical tips to help us in our goal of tasting the sweetness of prayer.

1. Create the Right Atmosphere

Whenever you can, give your prayer the attention it deserves. If you pray at home, prepare your room for prayer. After all, you will be standing in front of your Creator. Make sure your room is neat and clean. Add some nice fragrance. Have your own prayer niche that you can decorate in a beautiful and pleasant way. Have some prayer beads. Your Qur'an should be there as well. Make this space your mosque at home. You will see that it makes a huge difference to pray in such a space instead of just praying in the middle of the living room. If you pray the obligatory prayers in congregation in the mosque, make sure that you keep some *sunna* prayers to perform at home.

2. Have Your Special Prayer Clothes

Like creating your own prayer space, you should also have your special prayer clothes. Wearing these clothes after ablution will help you get into the right mode. Your focus will automatically be directed toward prayer and toward meeting your Lord in prayer. I usually wear a white prayer gown from Indonesia with some delicate embroideries. One of my teachers from Indonesia explained to me why she likes to wear a white prayer gown. She said that white reminds her of death, as we will be shrouded in white sheets after our soul has left our body. According to her, white is also one of the colors of Paradise. So she wants to be reminded of both death and Paradise during her prayer. I found that a beautiful practice.

3. Have the Proper Prayer Mat

This point might be irrelevant to some of you but for those who are easily distracted by visual forms, it is essential. Choose a prayer mat that doesn't distract you. My favorite prayer mat is a simple, plain golden-brown mat without any ornaments or visual elements. There is nothing that can distract my eyes or my mind.

4. Have Some Quiet Time Before Prayer

Several years ago, I was invited to talk about my conversion to a group of ladies. During the Q&A session, one lady took me by surprise with her question. She asked me how to improve concentration in prayer. She explained that she always thinks of other things during her prayer. I wasn't prepared for this kind of question as I had only recently started to learn more about drawing closer to Allah عَزَّوَجَلَّ. However, Allah inspired me to ask her what she did before her prayer. And she answered that she usually watches TV before praying.

By answering my question, she answered her own question: "Oh...now I understand. Watching TV before prayer is what distracts me from focusing on Allah."

It's not just watching TV. But our constant, immediate availability to be online through our phones is a huge distraction. If possible, we need to try to have some quiet time, some offline time before meeting our most merciful Creator.

5. Remember Allah Outside of Prayer

I would like to share one last point. It is absolutely essential that we remember Allah سُبْحَانَهُ وَتَعَالَى outside of our prayer as well. We need to remember Him as much as possible. Reading Qur'an. Doing *dhikr*. Pondering on Allah's signs in creation. Learning Islamic knowledge. Being in the company of pious believers. Try to remember Allah as much and as often as possible because Allah mentions in His Holy Qur'an those who remember Him standing and sitting, and lying on their sides.

> ... those who remember Allah standing and sitting, and [lying] on their sides, and ponder on the creation of the heavens and the earth [saying:] "Our Lord, You have not created all this in vain. We proclaim Your purity. So, save us from the punishment of Fire." (Qur'an 3:191)

May He make us of those who remember Him at all times, and may He make all of us of the righteous. *Ameen.*

Letter to the Beloved

This letter was written in response to an invitation by Sanad Collective and Dr. Tamara Gray from rabata.org to write a letter to our beloved Prophet Muhammad, may Allah bestow blessings and peace upon him. Other letters may be found at: https://www.instagram.com/letterstothebeloved

Dearest Prophet ﷺ,

Beloved father of my spiritual heart,

I bear witness that there is no God except Allah and that you are His last Messenger and Prophet.

I have wanted to write to you since your message reached me over ten years ago, but I did not know that this was even possible. There were so many things I wanted to tell you.

Dearest beloved Prophet,

May Allah, the All-Merciful, shower you with endless blessings and peace.

Whenever I look at the sun, I'm reminded of our most merciful Creator and of you because you brought the light of Islam. With your message, you brought us from darkness into the light, making

you the sun of my life. Allah took me out of layers and layers of darkness.

Dearest beloved Prophet and father of my spiritual heart,

May Allah ﷻ raise you to the most honorable position.

Whenever I look at the moon, I'm reminded of our most loving Creator and of you. You are the glowing hope in the darkness that still surrounds me sometimes. You are the cool calmness of my unsteady soul. Whenever I look at the moon, I'm reminded of Allah's miracle He gave to you. The splitting of the moon in your homeland, bringing complete conviction to some.

Oh Allah, because of your most beloved slave, protect our belief and grant us a good death.

I bear witness that there is no deity except Allah and that Muhammad is His last and final Messenger.

Dearest beloved Prophet and father of my spiritual heart,

May Allah bestow perfect blessings and peace upon you.

Whenever I witness Allah sending rain to earth, I'm reminded of our most merciful Creator, who created the heavens and the earth and everything in between. And I'm reminded of you, oh my Prophet.

Your message is the rain on my soul.

Your words are the rain on my heart.

Your words are the rain on my mind.

The rain of your words cleanses me.

The rain of your words refreshes me.

The rain of your words motivates me.

I bear witness that there is nothing worthy of worship except Allah and that Muhammad ibn Abdullah is His final Messenger.

Dearest beloved Prophet and father of my spiritual heart,

Every tree I pass reminds me of our most merciful Creator, who has blessed us with an amazing abundance of trees and plants. And my heart reminds me of you, oh father of my spiritual heart. You were the kindest to all creatures. You were sent as a mercy to the world. You were the kindest to animals, and you even showed utmost kindness, gentleness, and mercy to a tree trunk. Oh father of my spiritual heart!

I bear witness that there is nothing worthy of my worship except Allah and I bear witness that Muhammad is His slave and final Messenger.

Dearest and beloved Messenger and Prophet,

May Allah out of His infinite mercy make me meet you in His beautiful, eternal resting place—His Paradise.

Whenever I see a mountain, I'm reminded of Almighty Allah, who has created the mountains as peaks to give stability to this temporary world. And my heart reminds me of you, oh father of my spiritual heart. How Mount Uhud trembled under you, how you refused the riches and gold as big as Mount Uhud. And how you sought refuge in a cave in Mount Thawr, together with your companion, Abu Bakr.

Learning your words is my flight to the cave of knowledge. Learning your supplications is my flight to the cave of rest from this worldly life. Reading your life story is my flight to the cave of love for you. Oh father of my spiritual heart.

From the depths of my heart, I bear witness that there is absolutely nothing and nobody worthy of worship except Allah and that Muhammad is Allah's last and final Messenger.

Dearest and beloved Prophet of Allah, the All-mighty, the All-wise,

I ask Allah to shower abundant blessings and peace upon you, oh father of my spiritual heart.

When I look up to the sky and see uncountable stars, I'm reminded of our most benevolent Creator, who created the stars as a guide for the traveler and seafarer.

And every cell in my body reminds me of you, oh father of my spiritual heart, oh teachers of teachers, oh beloved Prophet.

You said that your honorable companions are the stars for us to follow after you left this temporary world. Oh Allah, guide us to the straight path.

I bear witness that there is no God but Allah and that Muhammad is His Messenger.

Dearest beloved Prophet and father of my spiritual heart,

May Allah ﻋَﺰَّوَجَلَّ shower peace and blessings on you.

Every time I look at my children. Every time I worry about my children's future. Every time I ask Allah to make them good Muslims.

I remember you, oh dearest Prophet.

I remember your words, your supplications to Allah: "*Ummati, Ummati*—my community, my community." Your concern for us.

Oh most beloved Prophet. Oh spiritual father. We ask for your intercession.

I'm your spiritual daughter.

Ya Allah, let me die a good death as your final Prophet's spiritual daughter.

I bear witness that there is nothing and nobody worthy of worship except Allah. And I bear witness that Muhammad is His slave and final Messenger.

Ya Allah, bestow the best and purest of blessings on our Prophet and send eternal peace upon him.

Dearest Prophet,

Please forgive my shortcomings. Please forgive my openness and bluntness. Please accept me as your spiritual daughter.

About the Author

Claudia Azizah Seise was born in 1983 in Germany and converted to Islam in 2008. Ever since then, she has aimed to study Islam and seek knowledge on becoming closer to God. One of her passions is supporting new and old converts to Islam. She obtained her PhD in Southeast Asian studies from Humboldt University Berlin, Germany, in 2016. From 2018 to 2019, she served as an assistant professor at the International Islamic University Malaysia. Besides her academic writings, she has been contributing to the German Islamic newspaper since 2008. Her poetry has been published in several collections. She also writes children's books. From September 2020 to December 2023, she was a postdoctoral fellow at the Berlin Institute of Islamic Theology, Germany.

Find her on Instagram: @clazahsei

www.ingramcontent.com/pod-product-compliance
Lightning Source LLC
Chambersburg PA
CBHW060601080526
44585CB00013B/652